THE NATIONAL MUSEUM OF
AFRICAN AMERICAN HISTORY AND CULTURE

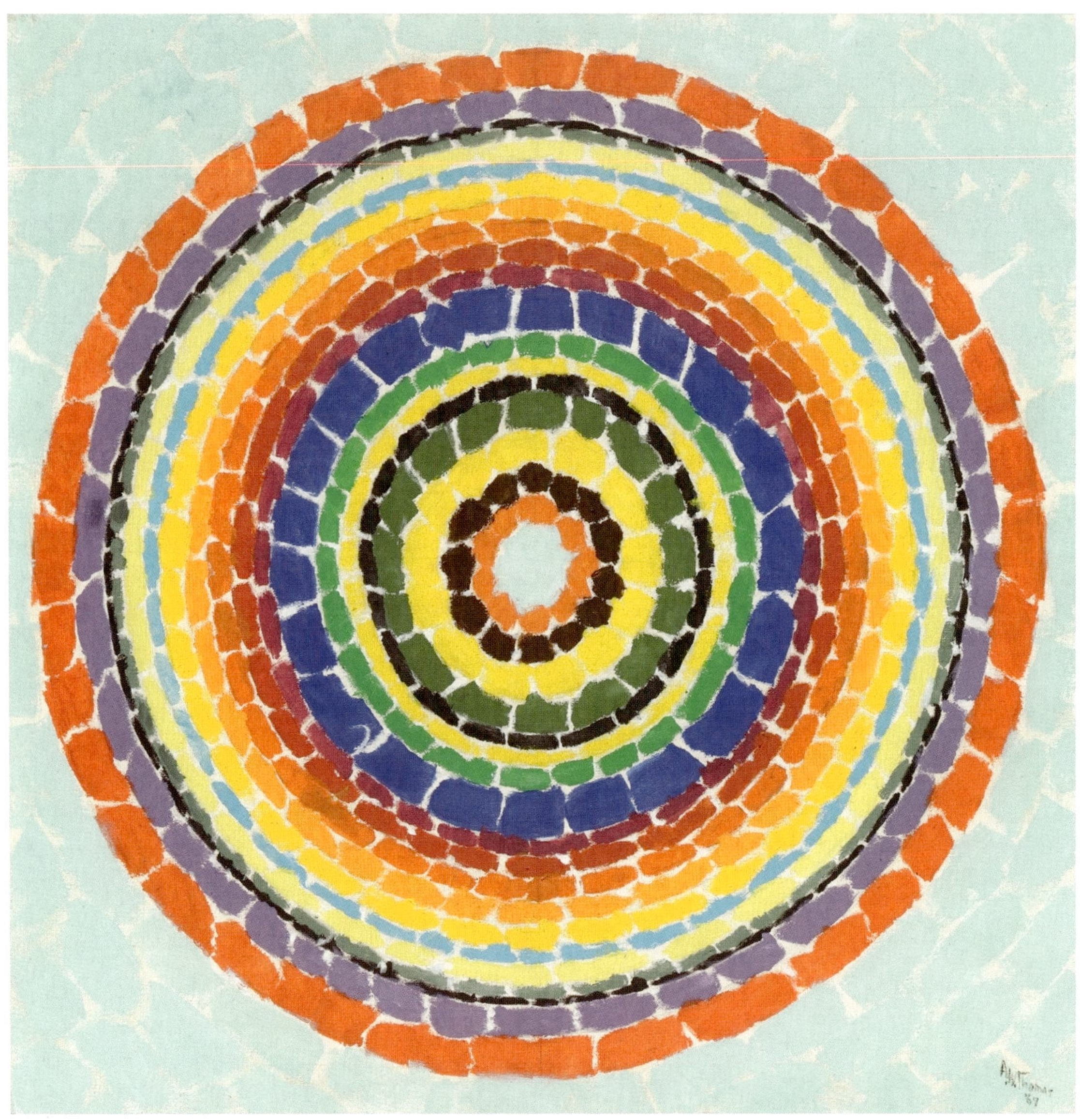

THE NATIONAL MUSEUM OF AFRICAN AMERICAN HISTORY AND CULTURE

A SOUVENIR BOOK

SECOND EDITION

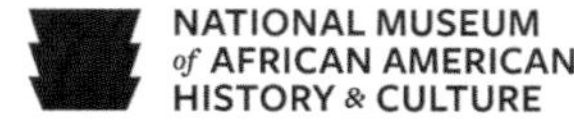

SMITHSONIAN BOOKS
WASHINGTON, DC

ABOUT THE MUSEUM

When the National Museum of African American History and Culture opened in 2016, it was the culmination of over one hundred years of efforts to document the living history of African Americans. Devoted to honoring and remembering African American life, history, and culture, it is a public institution open to all, where everyone is welcome to participate and learn.

When you walk into the monumental bronze building, Heritage Hall greets you. You descend to the 1400s, the time before modern slavery, then ascend through history to the present, exploring traditions of resilience, community, creativity, and more. The Museum provides continuity and context of African American life, where people from all walks of life see themselves and each other.

In the decade since it opened, the Museum's collection has grown to more than 45,000 objects. This second edition of our popular souvenir book features many of the iconic pieces that visitors have come to know and love alongside newly acquired highlights. The rich collection connects the past to the present, an ongoing effort as we think about the future, continuing this work and safeguarding this legacy for years to come.

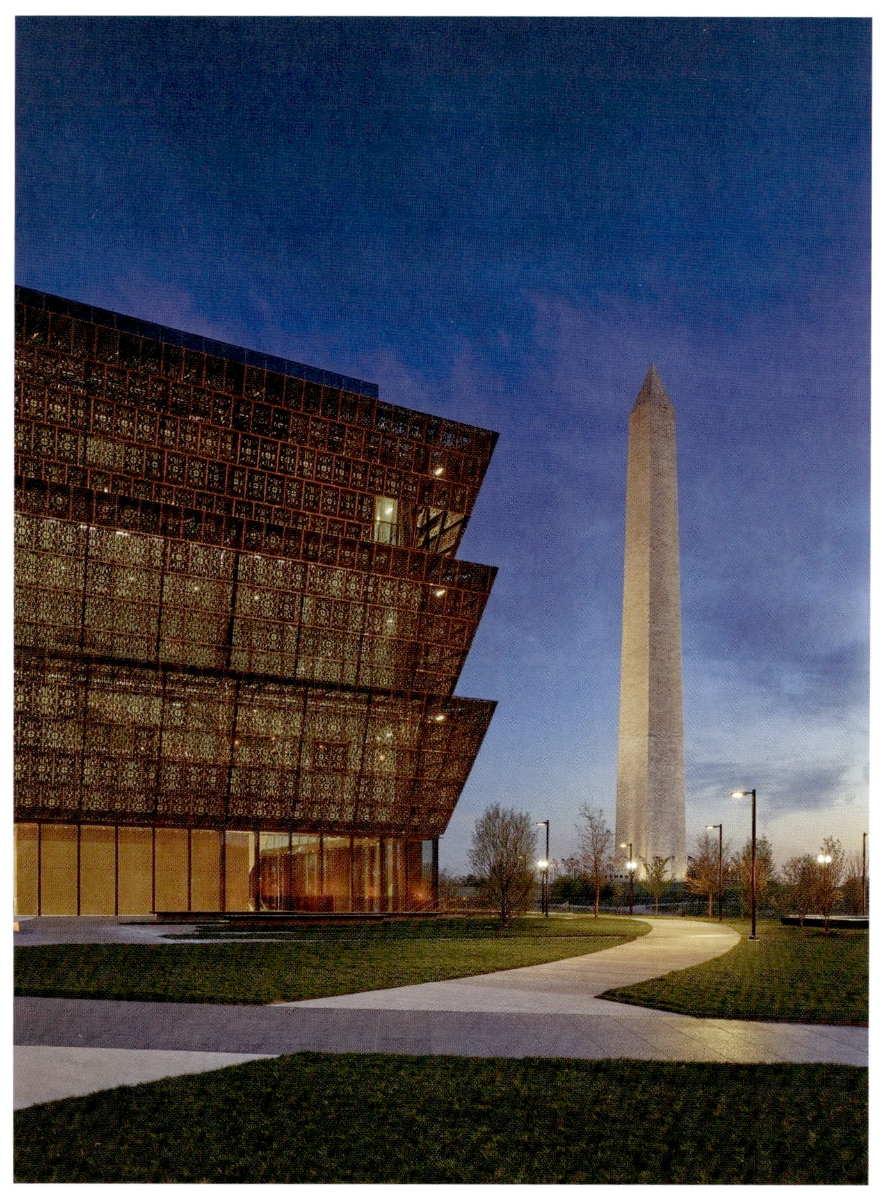

The Museum's architecture draws inspiration from the three-tiered crowns used in Yoruba art from West Africa, while the ornamental lattice pays homage to intricate ironwork once crafted by enslaved African Americans.

THE COLLECTION

When this museum was first created, many wondered if it would be possible to gather materials sufficient to establish a National Collection. Building a collection to represent "a people" is a challenge for any museum, and it seemed especially daunting given our nation's storied, yet complicated, history. However, African Americans have been documenting and collecting their history and culture since the 1800s, recognizing the need to save what others did not value. Building on these traditions, by the opening of the National Museum of African American History and Culture in 2016, the collection numbered more than 34,000 items. Since then, the Museum has increased its holdings to more than 45,000 objects—with the help of nearly six hundred and fifty new gifts by individual donors—ensuring a collection of national stature that helps us to explore the long arc of African American experience.

This sampling of the Museum's collection reveals the richness of African American material culture that has been gathered to explore that experience. Our goal has been to display iconic objects of African American history as well as to develop a strong photograph collection with documentary as well as artistic images. We have sought objects from famous individuals and the highest achievers in our culture, and also materials that reflect the experiences of ordinary people. By collecting art, we are illustrating the critical role that American artists of African descent have played in shaping the canon of American art.

James Baldwin stated, "American history is longer, larger, more various, more beautiful, and more terrible than anything anyone has ever said about it." What we begin to say with the stories in this museum is that African American history is American history. The objects here speak to each visitor in a unique way that helps all of us to understand the very human stories behind them.

MICHÈLE GATES MORESI
ASSISTANT DIRECTOR FOR COLLECTIONS

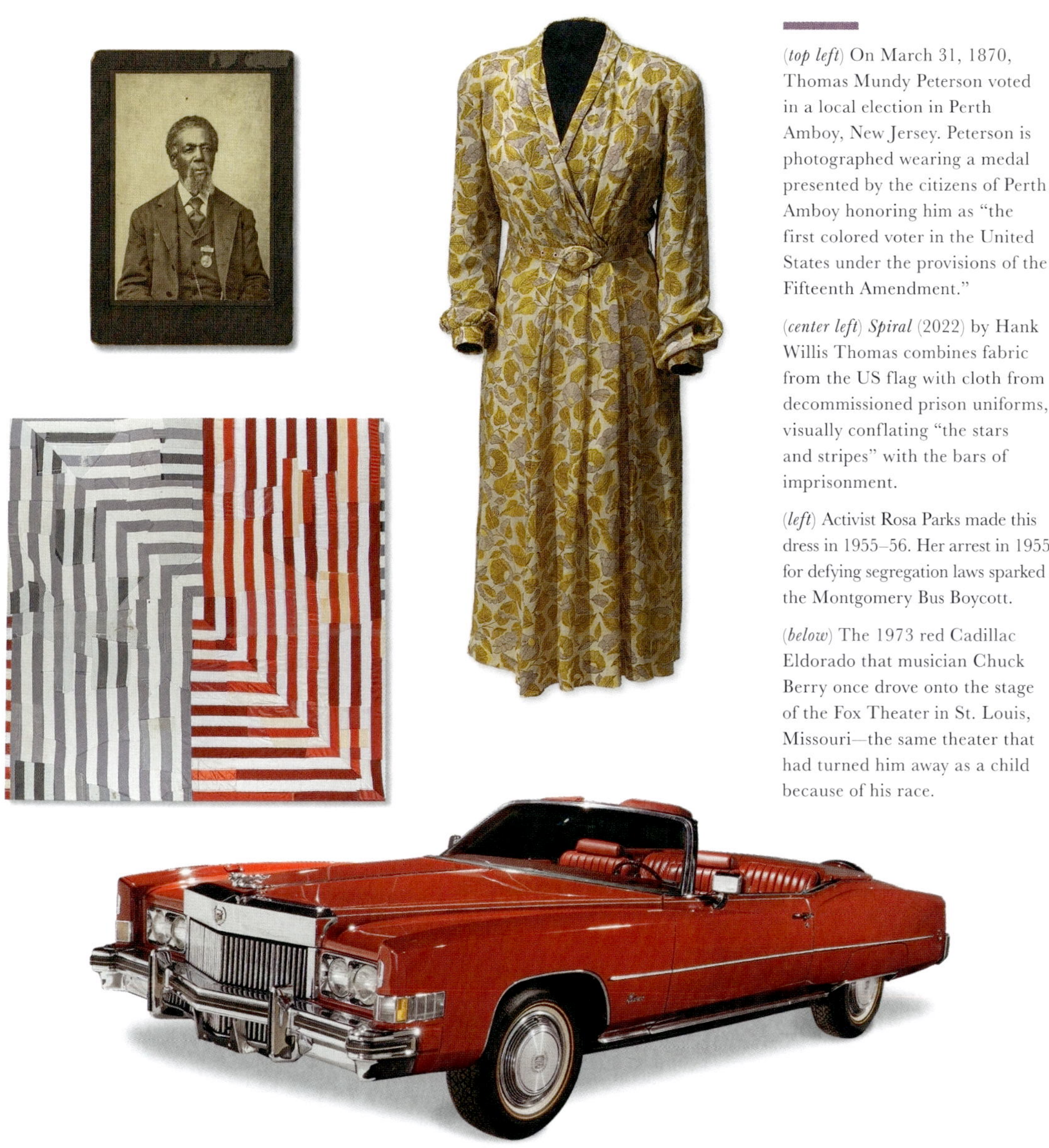

(*top left*) On March 31, 1870, Thomas Mundy Peterson voted in a local election in Perth Amboy, New Jersey. Peterson is photographed wearing a medal presented by the citizens of Perth Amboy honoring him as "the first colored voter in the United States under the provisions of the Fifteenth Amendment."

(*center left*) *Spiral* (2022) by Hank Willis Thomas combines fabric from the US flag with cloth from decommissioned prison uniforms, visually conflating "the stars and stripes" with the bars of imprisonment.

(*left*) Activist Rosa Parks made this dress in 1955–56. Her arrest in 1955 for defying segregation laws sparked the Montgomery Bus Boycott.

(*below*) The 1973 red Cadillac Eldorado that musician Chuck Berry once drove onto the stage of the Fox Theater in St. Louis, Missouri—the same theater that had turned him away as a child because of his race.

SLAVERY AND FREEDOM

Between 1619, when the first Africans arrived in Virginia, and 1865, when the Thirteenth Amendment abolishing slavery was passed, millions of African Americans spent their lives in bondage to other Americans, denied all rights to "life, liberty, and the pursuit of happiness."

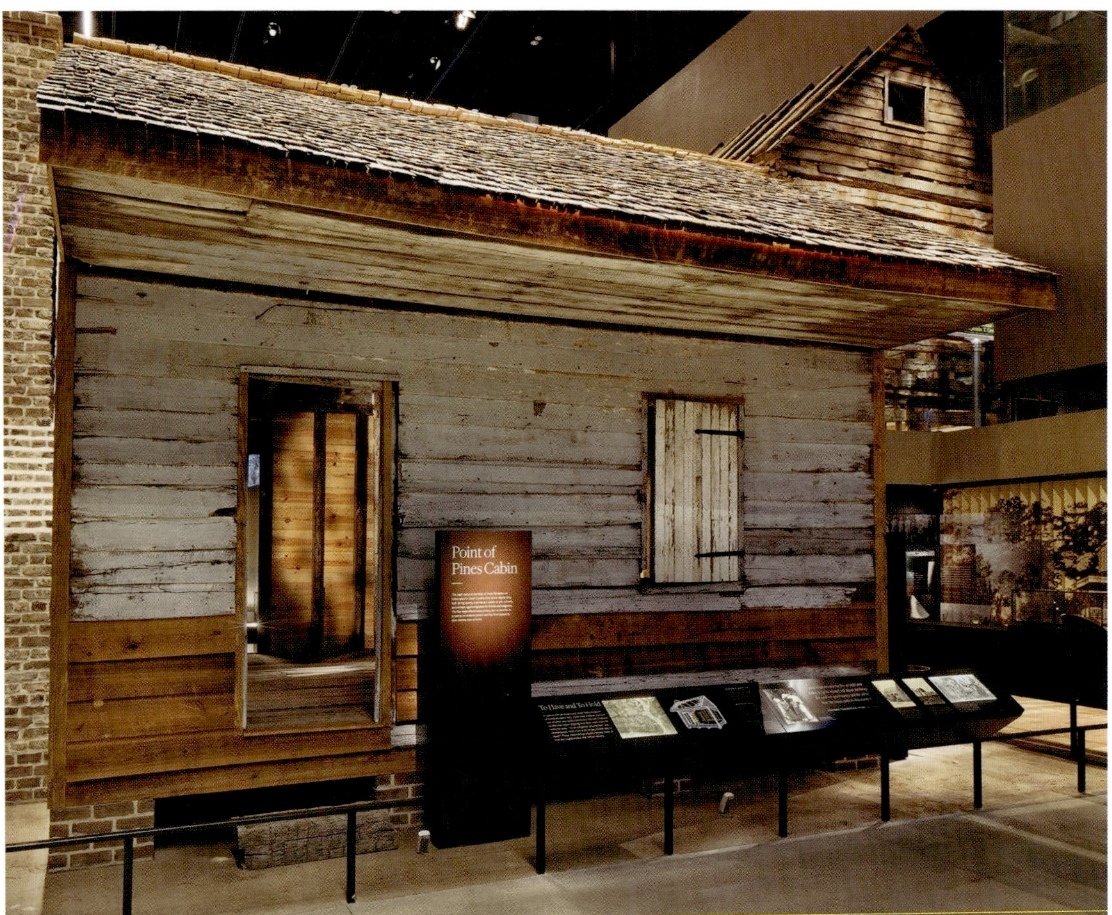

(*opposite*) This 150-year-old slave cabin from the Point of Pines Plantation on Edisto Island, South Carolina, was carefully dismantled, piece by piece, brought to the Museum, and reassembled in the *Slavery and Freedom* exhibition.

(*right*) The first African American to publish a volume of poetry, Phillis Wheatley is depicted on the frontispiece of this 1773 first edition of her work. She wrote the verses while still enslaved.

(*below*) "Freedom papers," like this 1852 Certificate of Freedom once carried by Joseph Trammel of Virginia, were carefully guarded by free African Americans in the South—hence the sturdy handmade metal box.

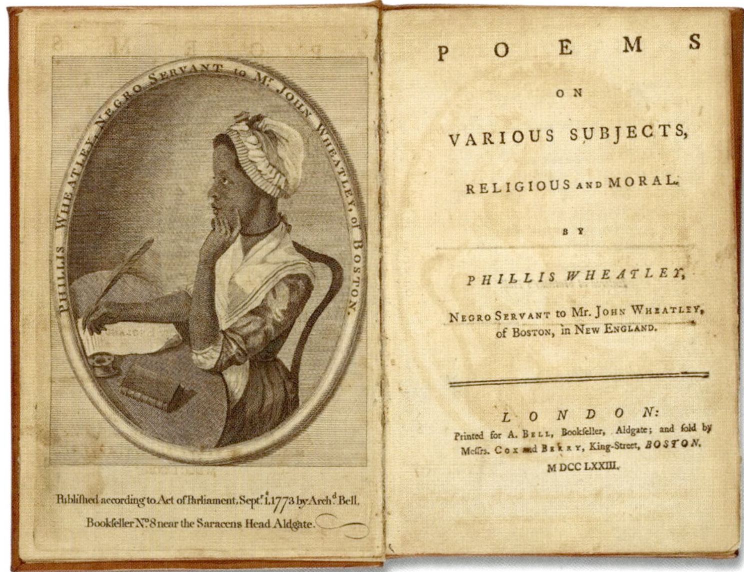

PHILLIS WHEATLEY, NEGRO SERVANT to Mr. JOHN WHEATLEY, of BOSTON.

Published according to Act of Parliament, Sept. 1, 1773 by Arch^d Bell. Bookseller No. 8 near the Saracens Head Aldgate.

POEMS ON VARIOUS SUBJECTS, RELIGIOUS AND MORAL.

BY

PHILLIS WHEATLEY,

NEGRO SERVANT to Mr. JOHN WHEATLEY, of BOSTON, in NEW ENGLAND.

LONDON:

Printed for A. BELL, Bookseller, Aldgate; and sold by Messrs. COX and BERRY, King-Street, BOSTON.

MDCCLXXIII.

(*below*) Enslavers in Charleston, South Carolina, who hired out enslaved laborers, had to outfit them with identification badges stating their occupation and the year (here, "fisher" and "1800").

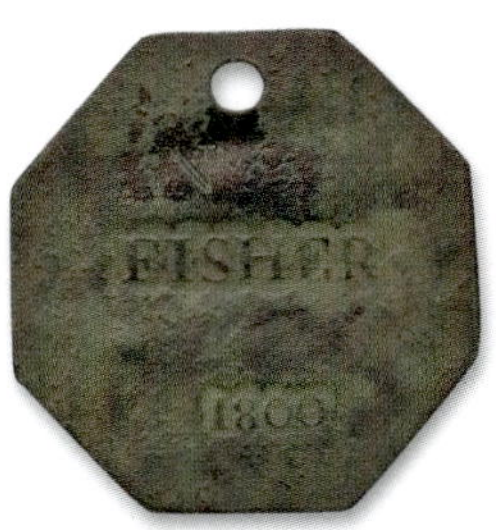

PETER BENTZON

Peter Bentzon was not only a free man, he was also a silversmith and jeweler who worked in Philadelphia and on the Caribbean Island of St. Croix. Bentzon was the first silversmith of African descent working in the United States to be recognized with his own mark.

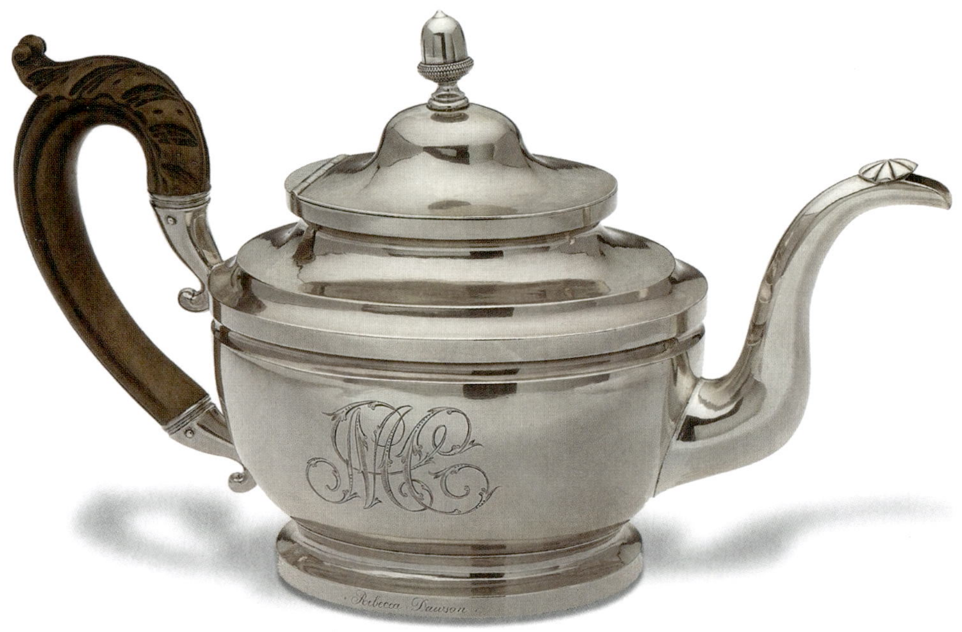

This exquisite silver teapot with an acorn finial, which Bentzon crafted between 1817 and 1829 in Philadelphia, was hand molded.

DAVID DRAKE

A rarity in antebellum South Carolina, the enslaved, yet literate, master craftsman David Drake, more commonly known as Dave the Potter, often signed, dated, and wrote verses on his pots—in an era when enslaved people were forbidden to read and write.

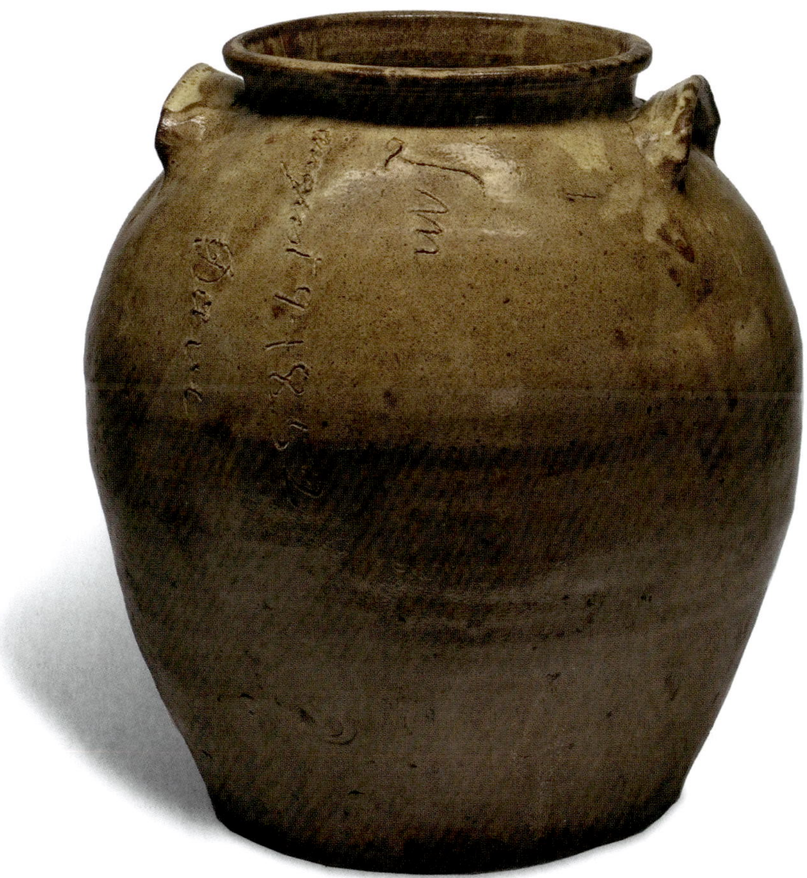

This large stoneware storage jar is signed by its maker, "Dave," and dated 1852.

ANTI-SLAVERY MOVEMENT

The movement to end slavery in the United States was led by white and Black men and women. While some sought stopping the practice by any means necessary, including violence, others advocated abolishing slavery based on moral grounds and aimed to change the Constitution.

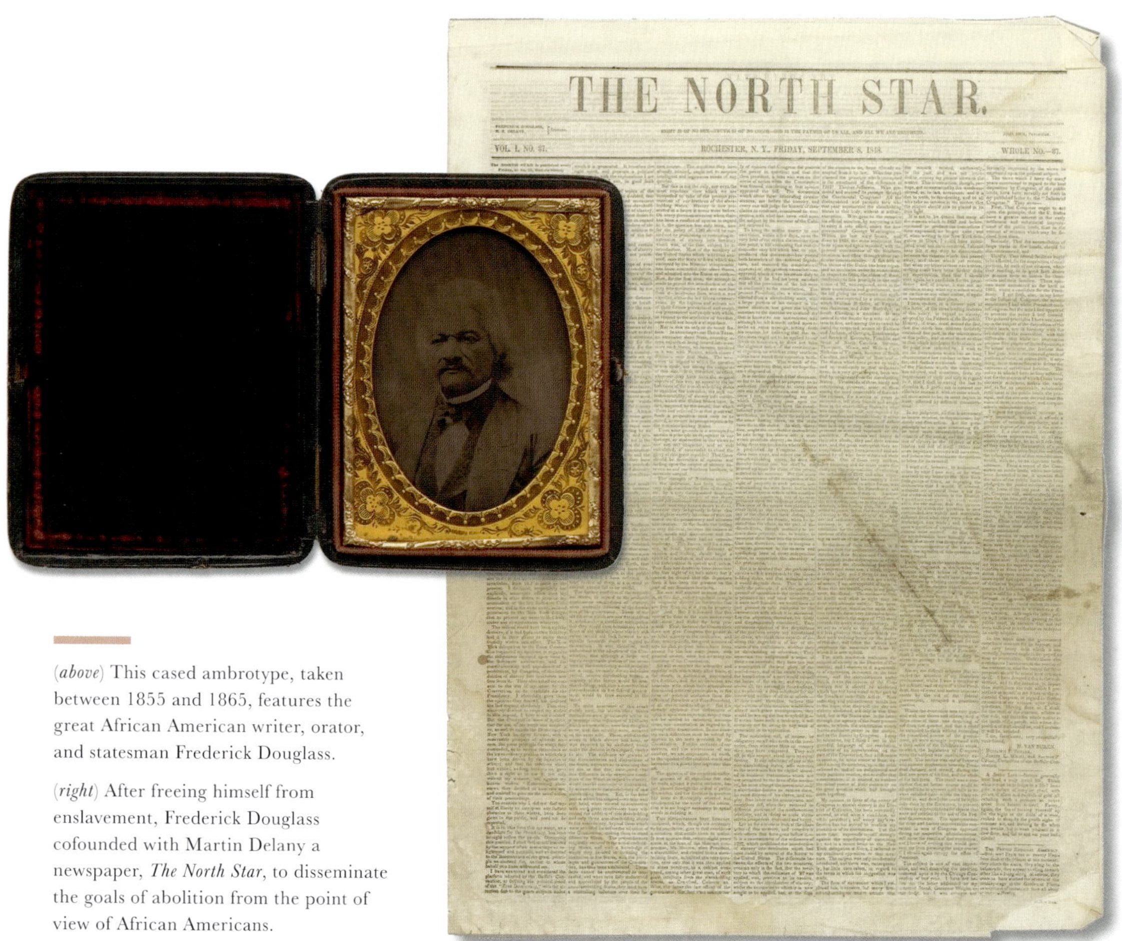

THE NORTH STAR.

VOL. I. NO. 37. ROCHESTER, N. Y., FRIDAY, SEPTEMBER 8, 1848. WHOLE NO.—37.

(*above*) This cased ambrotype, taken between 1855 and 1865, features the great African American writer, orator, and statesman Frederick Douglass.

(*right*) After freeing himself from enslavement, Frederick Douglass cofounded with Martin Delany a newspaper, *The North Star*, to disseminate the goals of abolition from the point of view of African Americans.

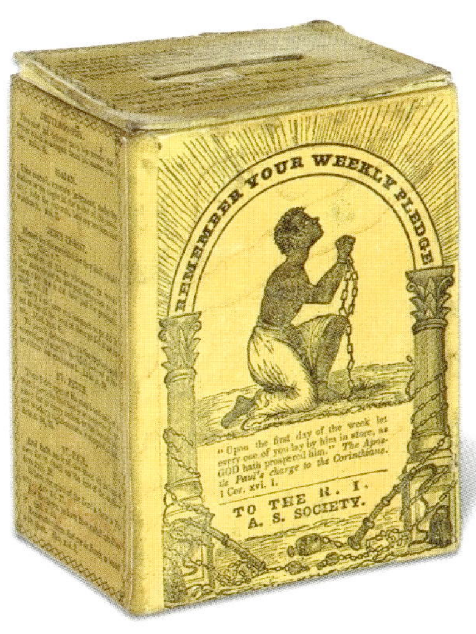

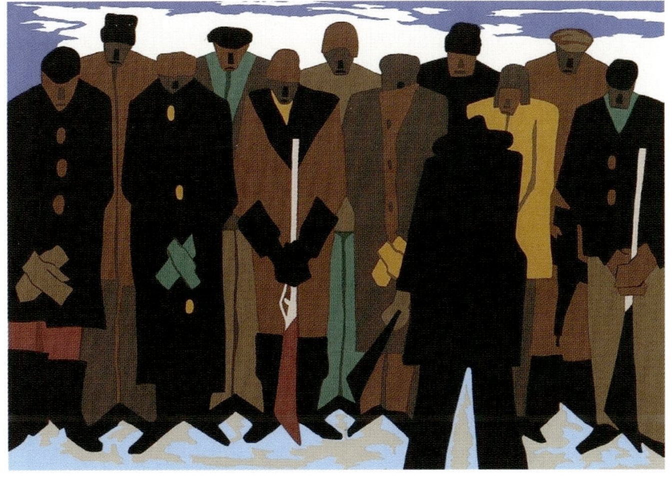

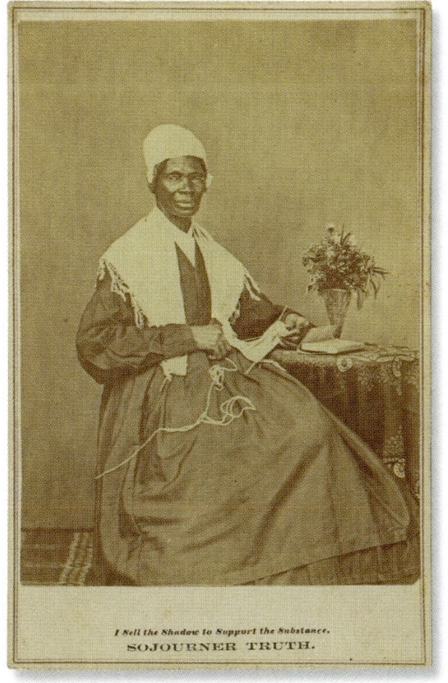

(*above left*) Surrounded by symbols of bondage, an enslaved man is depicted on a coin collection box used by the Garrison family for contributions to the Rhode Island Anti-Slavery Society.

(*left*) Sojourner Truth was an abolitionist and advocate of women's rights.

(*above*) Inspired by his own 1941 paintings, artist Jacob Lawrence created this screenprint series in 1977 depicting the lifelong quest of John Brown to end slavery in the United States.

HARRIET TUBMAN

Born enslaved in Maryland in 1822, Harriet Tubman escaped to the North but soon made the first of thirteen trips back to her native state, smuggling scores of family members and friends to freedom. During the Civil War, she led a raid that liberated seven hundred enslaved people.

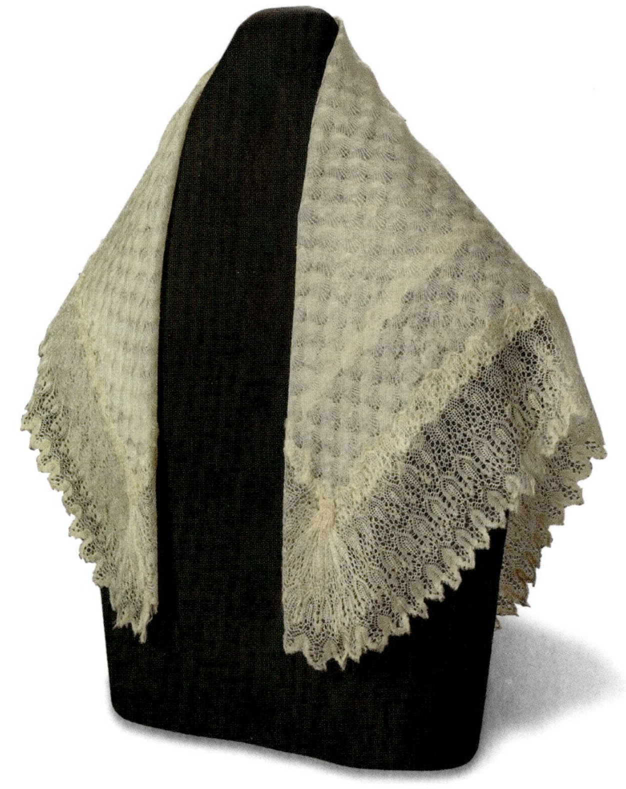

Britain's Queen Victoria so admired Harriet Tubman's audacity and dedication that she sent Tubman this silk and lace shawl around 1897.

This earliest known photograph of Harriet Tubman was taken in Auburn, New York, shortly after the end of the Civil War.

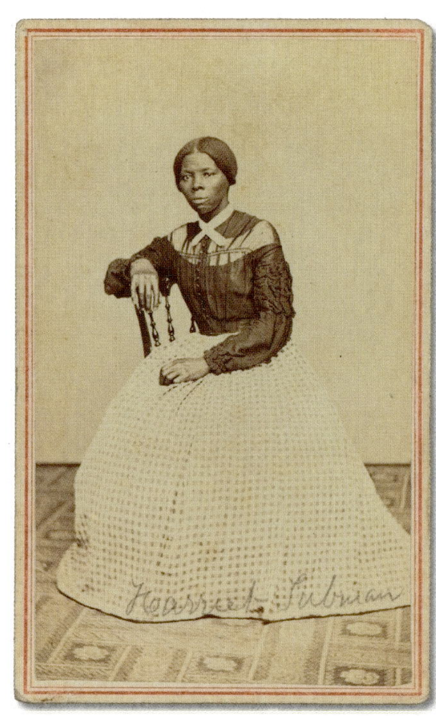

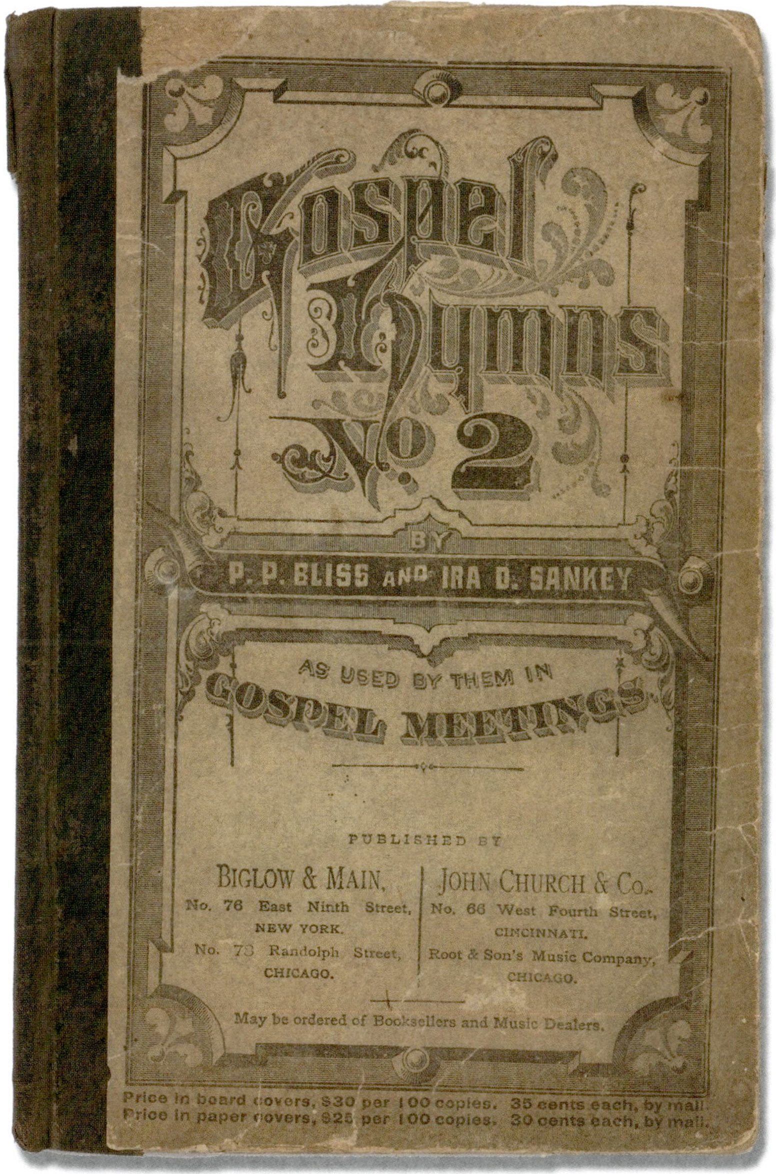

Although she could neither read nor write, Tubman was intensely devout and prized this, her personal hymnal.

THE CIVIL WAR

After President Lincoln issued the Emancipation Proclamation in 1863, the federal government began recruiting among free and formerly enslaved Black people in the North. By the end of the war, almost 200,000 African Americans were serving in the Union army—nearly 10 percent of its strength.

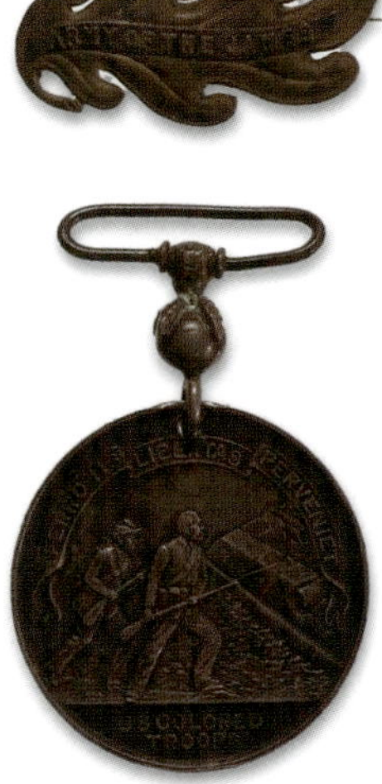

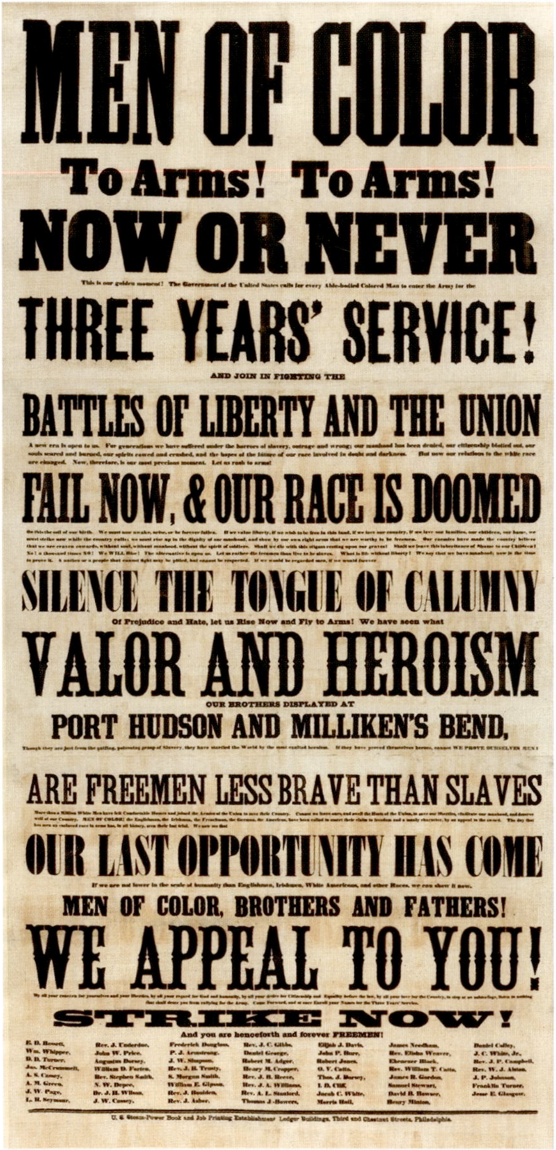

(*above*) The Army of the James Medal was commissioned by General Benjamin F. Butler to honor African American troops who fought with valor at the Battle of New Market Heights, Virginia, on September 29, 1864. The Latin inscription means "Freedom will be theirs by the sword."

(*right*) The citizens of Philadelphia could not fail to miss this eight-by-four-foot bill from June 1863 signed by Frederick Douglass and fifty-three others, with its ringing appeals to "men of color" to join the fight.

MEN OF COLOR

To Arms! To Arms!

NOW OR NEVER

This is our golden moment! The Government of the United States calls for every Able-bodied Colored Man to enter the Army for the

THREE YEARS' SERVICE!

AND JOIN IN FIGHTING THE

BATTLES OF LIBERTY AND THE UNION

A new era is open to us. For generations we have suffered under the horrors of slavery, outrage and wrong; our manhood has been denied, our citizenship blotted out, our souls seared and burned, our spirits cowed and crushed, and the hopes of the future of our race involved in doubt and darkness. But now our relations to the white race are changed. Now, therefore, is our most precious moment. Let us rush to arms!

FAIL NOW, & OUR RACE IS DOOMED

SILENCE THE TONGUE OF CALUMNY

Of Prejudice and Hate, let us Rise Now and Fly to Arms! We have seen what

VALOR AND HEROISM

OUR BROTHERS DISPLAYED AT

PORT HUDSON AND MILLIKEN'S BEND,

ARE FREEMEN LESS BRAVE THAN SLAVES

OUR LAST OPPORTUNITY HAS COME

If we are not lower in the scale of humanity than Englishmen, Irishmen, White Americans, and other Races, we can show it now.

MEN OF COLOR, BROTHERS AND FATHERS!

WE APPEAL TO YOU!

STRIKE NOW!

And you are henceforth and forever FREEMEN!

E. D. Bassett,	Rev. J. Underdue,	Frederick Douglass,	Rev. J. C. Gibbs,	Elijah J. Davis,	James Needham,	Daniel Colley,
Wm. Whipper,	John W. Price,	P. J. Armstrong,	Daniel George,	John P. Burr,	Rev. Elisha Weaver,	J. C. White, Jr.,
D. D. Turner,	Augustus Dorsey,	J. W. Simpson,	Robert M. Adger,	Robert Jones,	Ebenezer Black,	Rev. J. P. Campbell,
Jas. McCrummell,	William D. Forten,	Rev. J. B. Trusty,	Henry M. Cropper,	O. V. Catto,	Rev. William T. Catto,	Rev. W. J. Alston,
A. S. Cassey,	Rev. Stephen Smith,	S. Morgan Smith,	Rev. J. B. Reeve,	Thos. J. Dorsey,	James R. Gordon,	J. P. Johnson,
A. M. Green,	N. W. Depee,	William E. Gipson,	Rev. J. A. Williams,	I. D. Cliff,	Samuel Stewart,	Franklin Turner,
J. W. Page,	Dr. J. H. Wilson,	Rev. J. Boulden,	Rev. A. L. Stanford,	Jacob C. White,	David B. Bowser,	Jesse E. Glasgow,
L. R. Seymour,	J. W. Cassey,	Rev. J. Asher,	Thomas J. Bowers,	Morris Hall,	Henry Minton,	

U. S. Steam-Power Book and Job Printing Establishment, Ledger Buildings, Third and Chestnut Streets, Philadelphia.

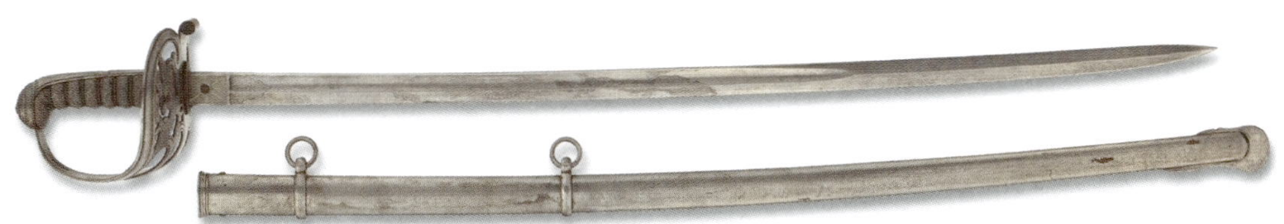

(*above*) This etched Mameluke sword and scabbard were presented to Captain George Thompson Garrison, son of abolitionist William Lloyd Garrison, by the 55th Massachusetts Volunteer Infantry, the state's second regiment of African American volunteers. Its officers were white; its enlisted men were Black.

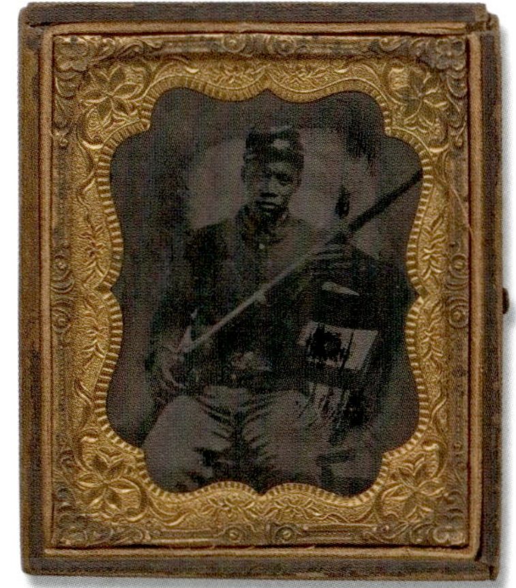

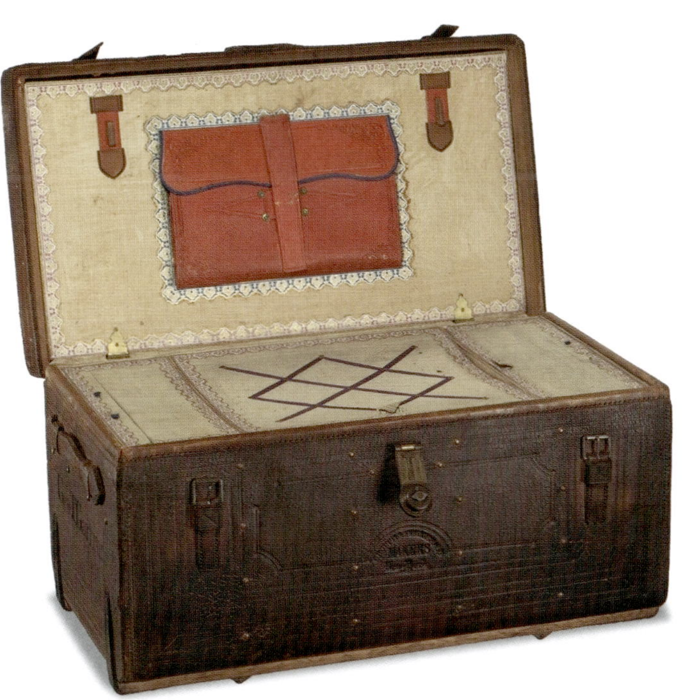

(*above*) Qualls Tibbs, a sergeant in the 27th Infantry Regiment of the United States Colored Troops, was wounded during the war, but he survived and lived until 1922.

(*left*) Captain George Thompson Garrison, who fought with the 55th Massachusetts, owned this travel trunk. When Charleston, South Carolina, fell in February 1865, he led his soldiers into the captured city, all of them singing "John Brown's Body," a marching song about the abolitionist.

EMANCIPATION AND RECONSTRUCTION

In 1865, the Civil War ended, Congress passed the Thirteenth Amendment abolishing slavery, and the nation embarked upon the Reconstruction era (ca. 1865–77). African Americans in the South, many of them newly freed, were able to vote, and Black people were elected to state and national offices.

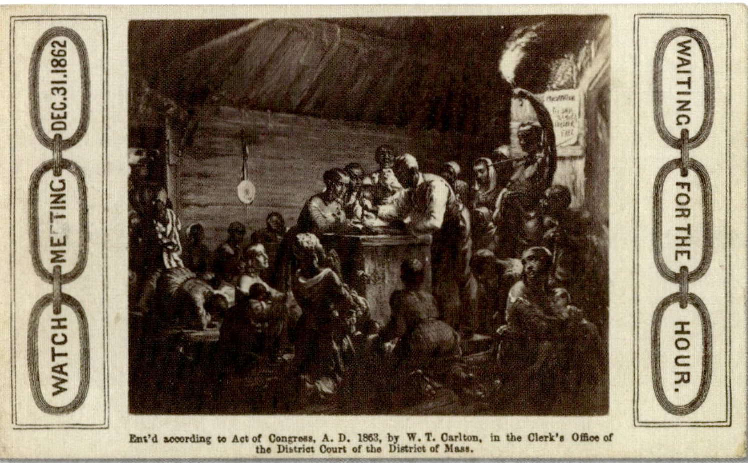

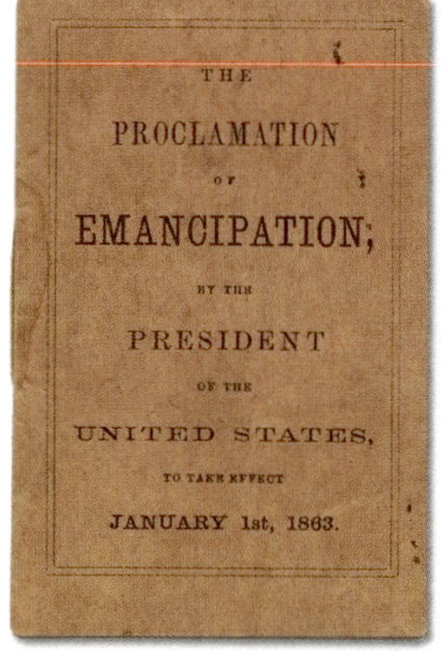
THE
PROCLAMATION
OF
EMANCIPATION;
BY THE
PRESIDENT
OF THE
UNITED STATES,
TO TAKE EFFECT
JANUARY 1st, 1863.

(*above*) This pocket-sized Emancipation Proclamation was produced specifically for Union soldiers to bring word of emancipation to African Americans.

(*above*) Known as Watch Night, on December 31, 1862, African Americans gathered in churches and homes to await the moment the Emancipation Proclamation went into effect.

(*right*) Elizabeth Keckly, the personal dressmaker to First Lady Mary Todd Lincoln, is believed to have made this pair of stars-and-stripes crocheted slippers for Secretary of the Navy Gideon Welles.

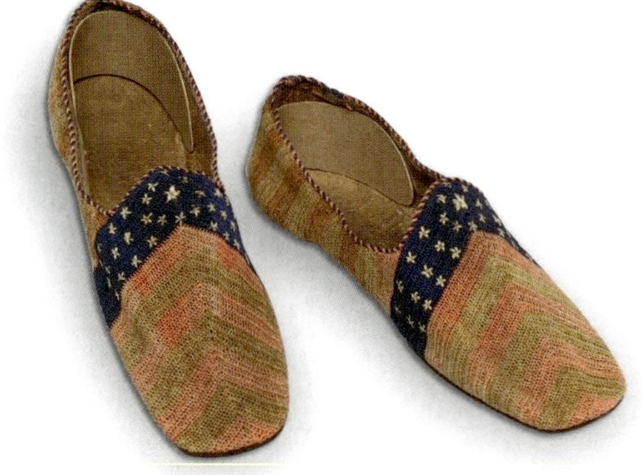

(*right*) This campaign button features Senator William B. Nash, a formerly enslaved worker at Hunt's Hotel in Columbia, South Carolina, who served in the South Carolina state senate from 1868 to 1877.

(*below*) During the Reconstruction period, hundreds of schools like this Freedmen's School in New Bern, North Carolina, were established by African American communities with teachers and supplies provided by the Freedmen's Bureau and Northern aid societies.

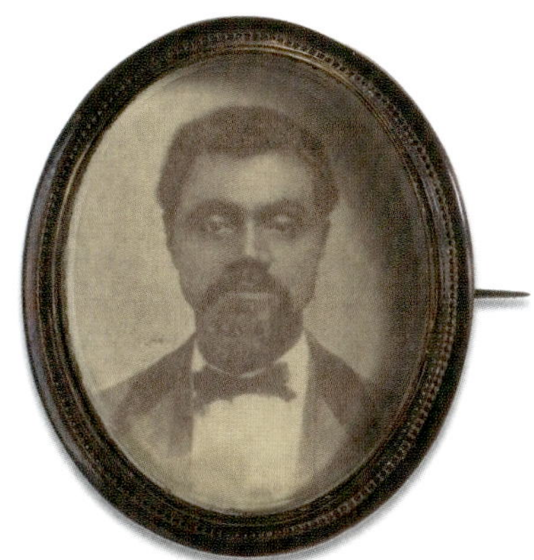

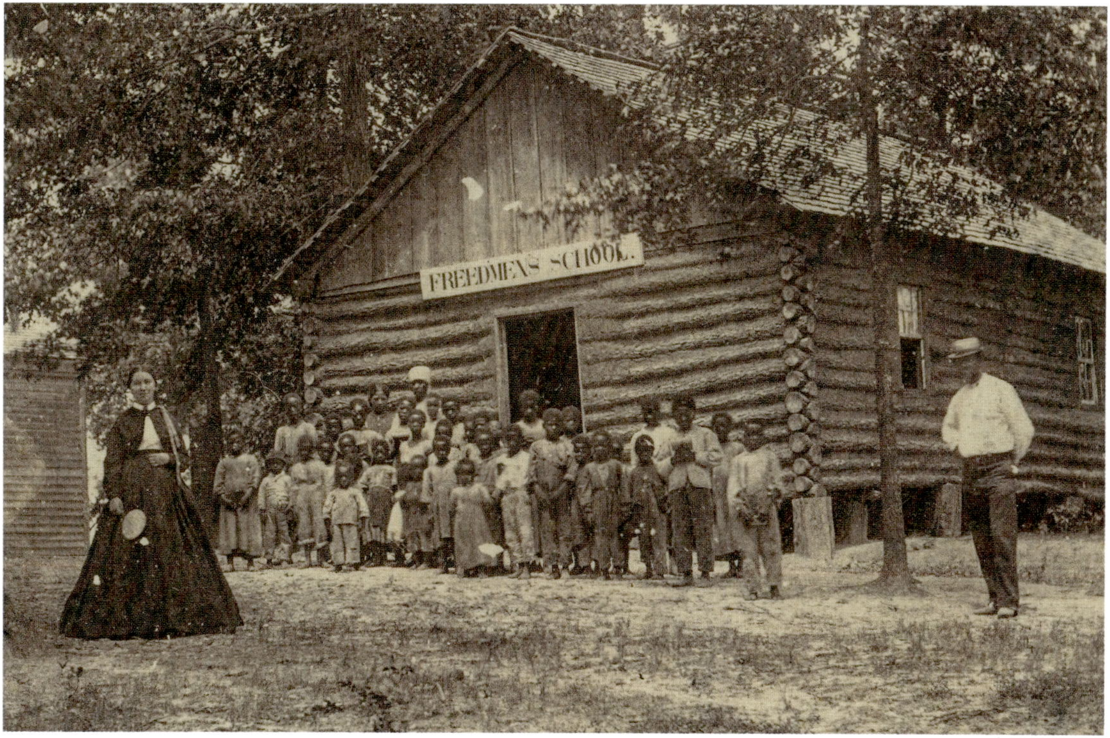

SEGREGATION

With the end of slavery, African Americans had hoped to attain full citizenship. Instead, they found themselves resisting efforts to put in place a new form of oppression—segregation. Through struggle and perseverance, African Americans challenged the nation to live up to its ideals of freedom and equality.

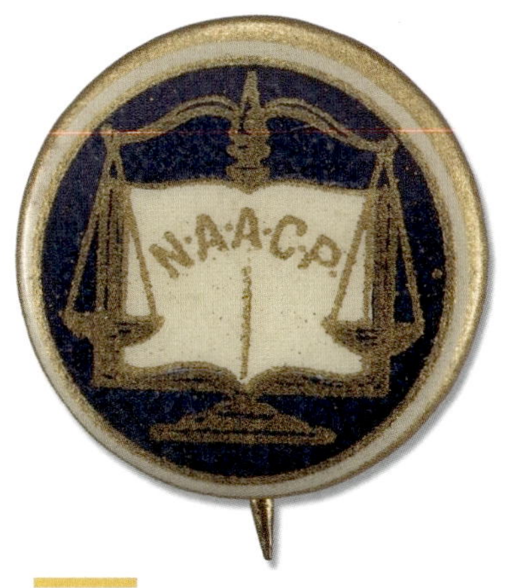

The National Association for the Advancement of Colored People (NAACP) was formed in 1909 to lead efforts against racial segregation and disenfranchisement.

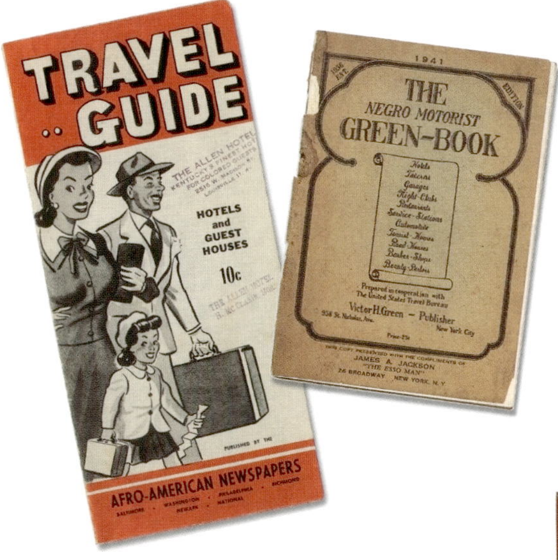

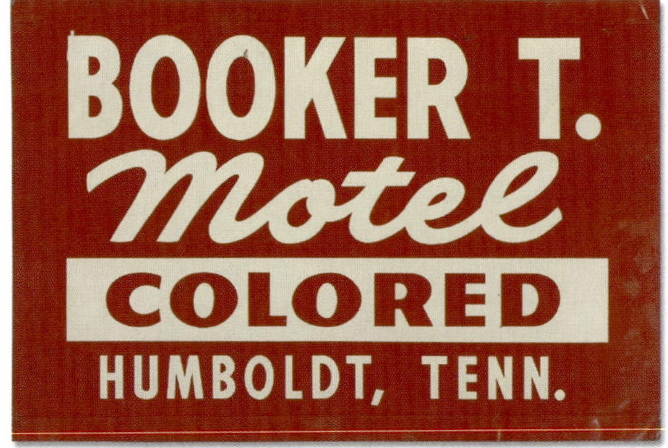

(*above*) Travel guides like these, often referred to as "Green Books" after the popular *The Negro Motorist Green-Book* (1936–67) by Victor H. Green, were essential for Black vacationers and travelers looking for safe services and accommodations during segregation.

(*right*) By plainly indicating that Black guests were welcome, Black-owned motels like the Booker T. took the guesswork out of deciding where to stay when traveling by automobile.

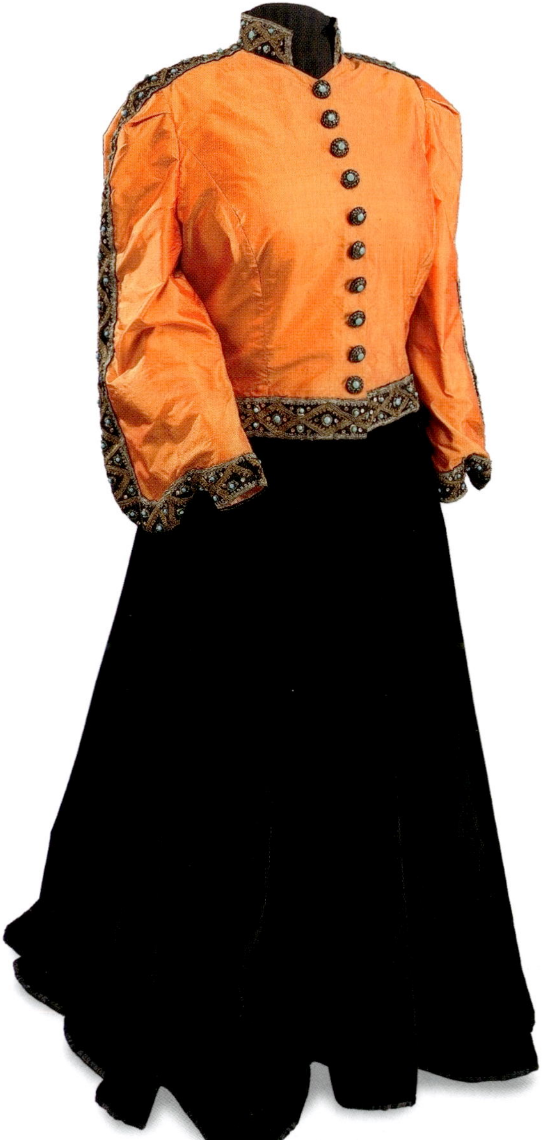

(*left*) Marian Anderson wore this ensemble (modified in 1993) when she gave her famous concert on the steps of the Lincoln Memorial in Washington, DC, in 1939.

(*below*) This clock made of wood, copper, plastic, and metal also features the stained-glass sign of the Citizens Savings and Trust Company, the nation's oldest continuously operated African American bank.

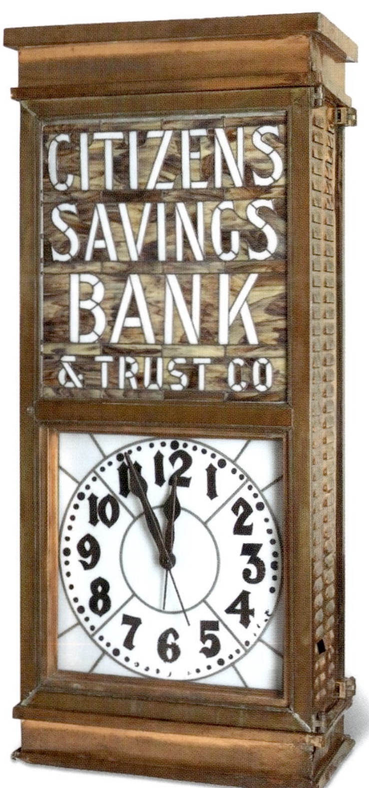

WOMEN'S CLUBS

Black women worked in their communities to improve the social, economic, and political status of African Americans. Women organized their efforts on a national level, starting with the National Association of Colored Women's Clubs (NACW) in 1896. Later, with the leadership of Mary McLeod Bethune in 1935, the National Council of Negro Women (NCNW) aimed to unite and channel the activities of women's organizations across the country.

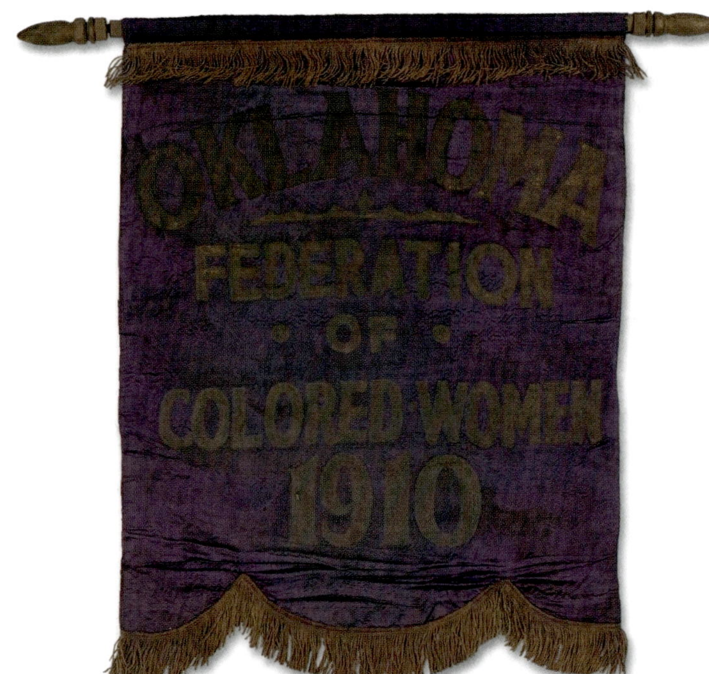

This banner was used by the Oklahoma Federation of Colored Women's Clubs, which promoted education, self-help, and support for Black communities.

Mary Church Terrell, an activist for education and civil rights, was the first president of the NACW. This portrait by Addison Scurlock accompanied the column she wrote for the *Chicago Defender*.

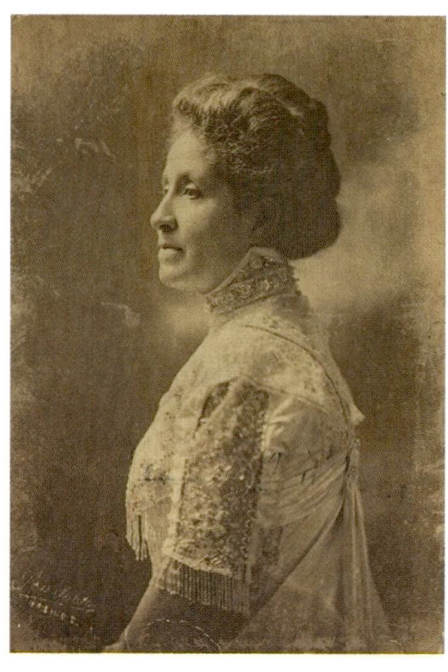

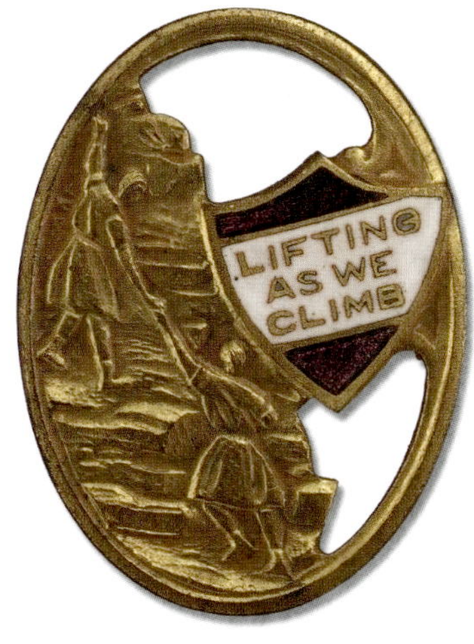

This pin worn by Mary Church Terrell features the NACW motto, "Lifting as we climb," representing the organization's goal to bring each generation a step closer to equality and social justice.

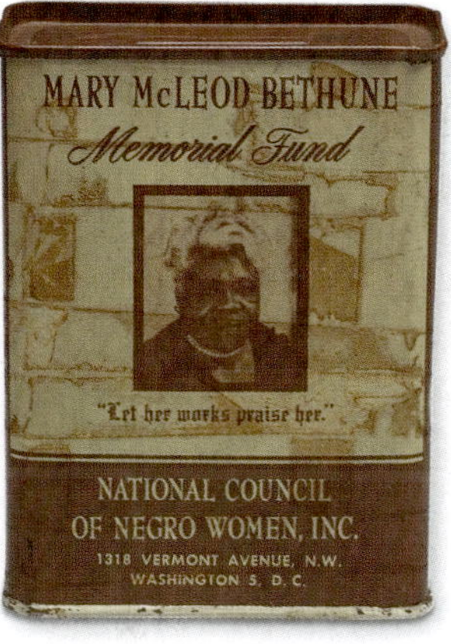

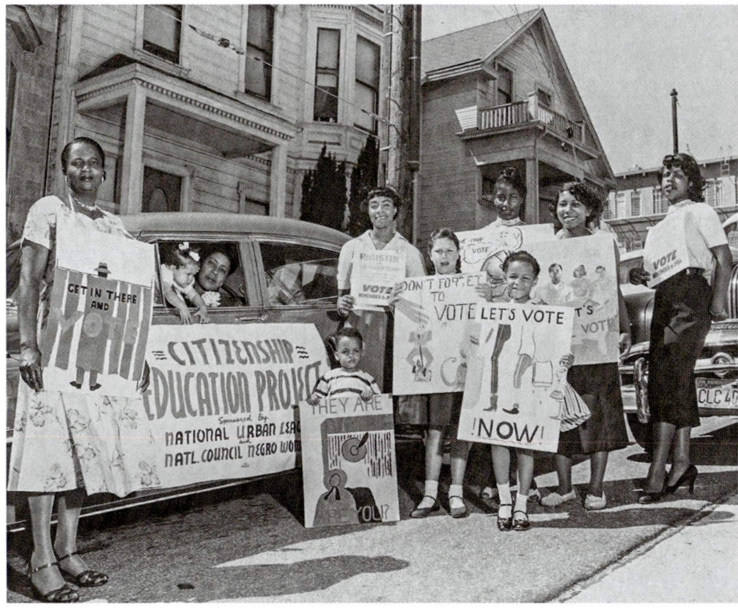

(*above*) The NCNW raised funds to establish a memorial honoring founder Mary McLeod Bethune, whose tireless work helped lay the foundation for the Civil Rights Movement.

(*left*) In 1956, Frances Albrier, president of the San Francisco Chapter of the NCNW, compiled a scrapbook featuring photographs and clippings documenting the chapter's voter registration efforts.

PULLMAN PORTERS

In the early twentieth century, a job as a Pullman porter meant status for African American men. Although catering to passenger needs in the famous sleeping cars could be menial, the wages were good, and the Brotherhood of Sleeping Car Porters was a powerful and protective Black labor union.

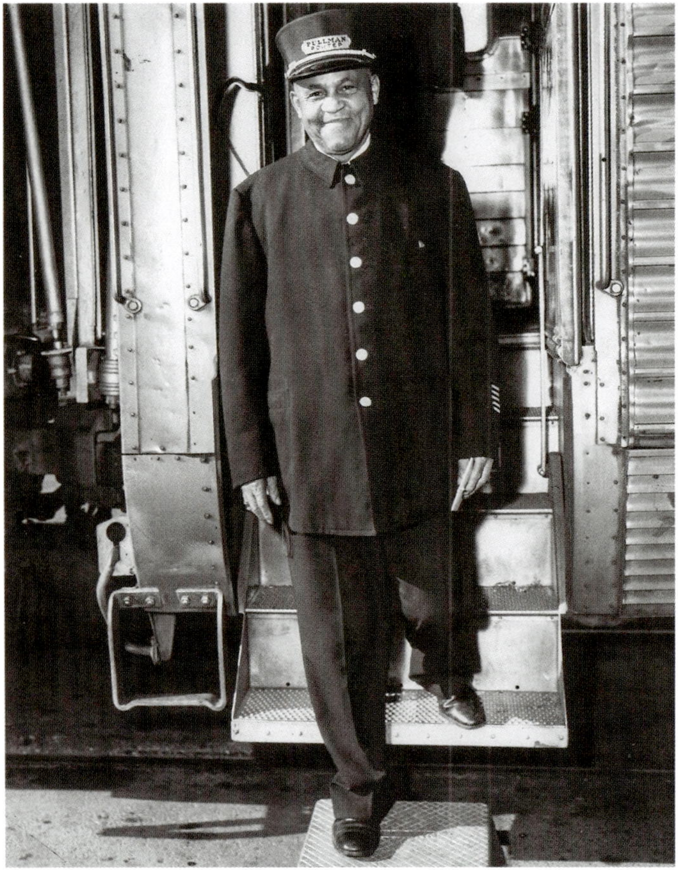

(*left*) Pullman porters greeted train passengers for decades. James Bryant, seen standing here on the steps of a Pullman sleeper, worked at the Pullman Company from 1928 to 1973.

(*below*) Porters placed step stools such as this one at each stop to assist passengers climbing down from the cars.

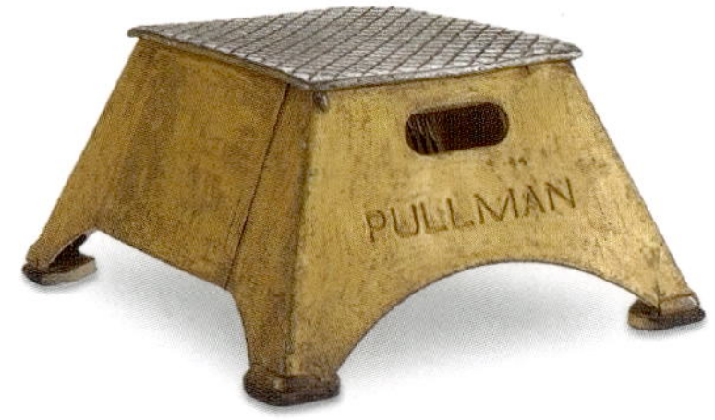

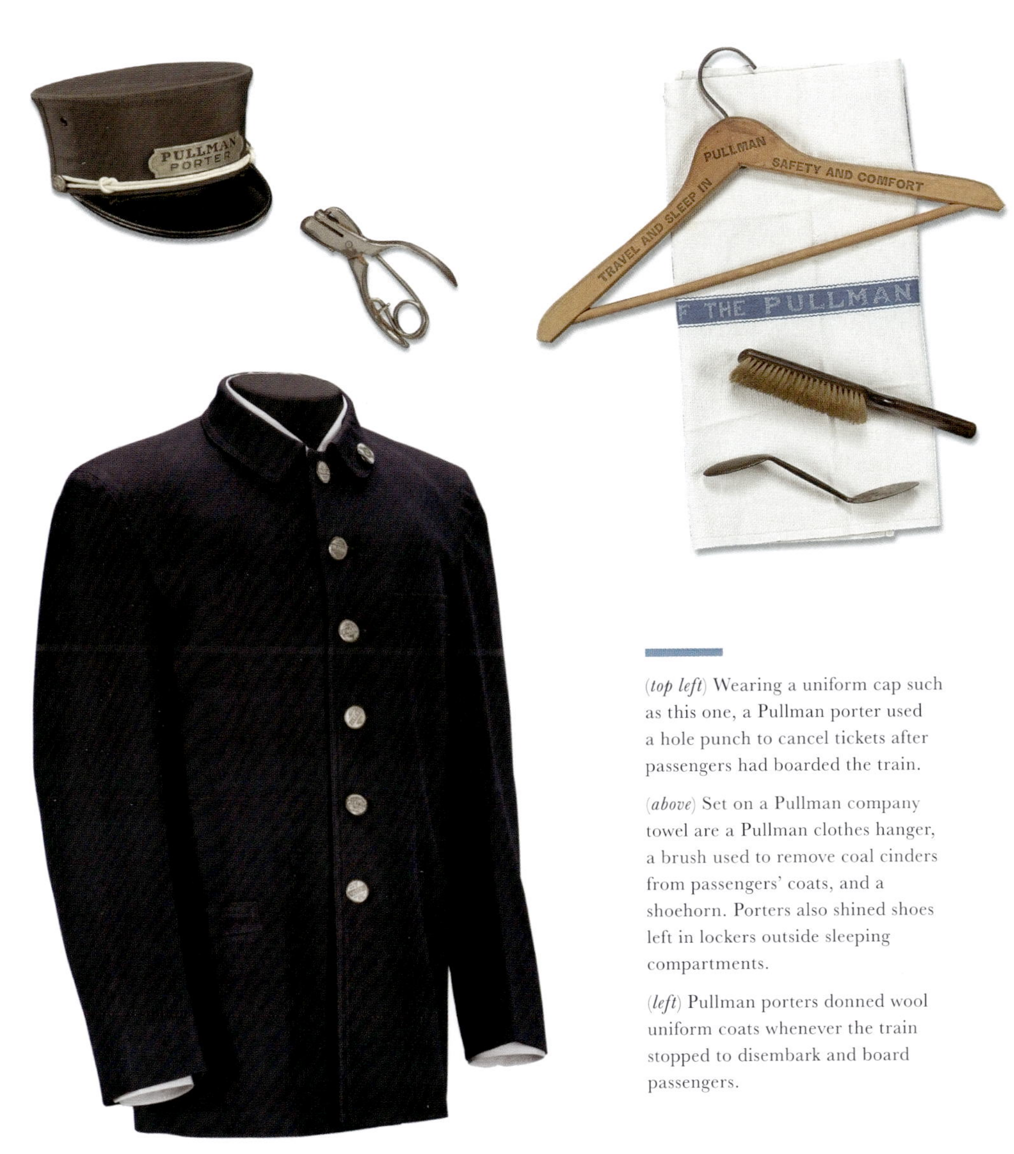

(*top left*) Wearing a uniform cap such as this one, a Pullman porter used a hole punch to cancel tickets after passengers had boarded the train.

(*above*) Set on a Pullman company towel are a Pullman clothes hanger, a brush used to remove coal cinders from passengers' coats, and a shoehorn. Porters also shined shoes left in lockers outside sleeping compartments.

(*left*) Pullman porters donned wool uniform coats whenever the train stopped to disembark and board passengers.

SEGREGATED RAILCAR

Built by the Pullman Palace Car Company and owned and operated by Southern Railway, car no. 1200 ran as a long-distance passenger coach between Washington, DC, and New Orleans, Louisiana, in the 1940s and 1950s. Operating separate passenger cars for Black and white people was expensive, so railcars such as this one were reconfigured to create partitioned "white" and "colored" sections to oblige Jim Crow segregation in the South. African Americans repeatedly challenged state-mandated separate accommodations in the nineteenth and twentieth centuries, both before and after the Supreme Court upheld the "separate but equal" doctrine in *Plessy v. Ferguson* (1896). A string of legal challenges brought before the Interstate Commerce Commission and the Supreme Court between 1940 and 1960 paved the way for the end of segregated interstate trains and buses.

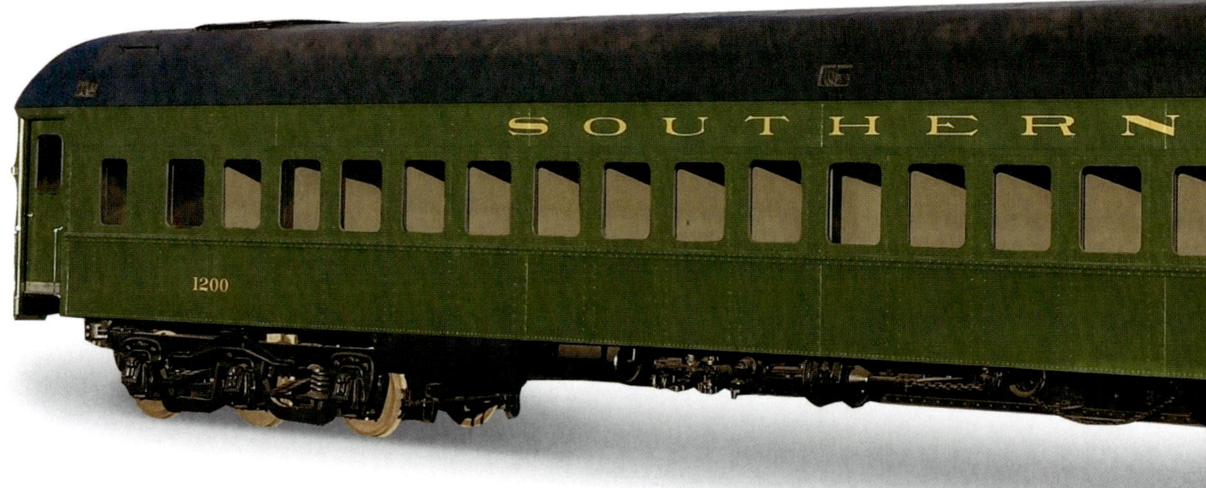

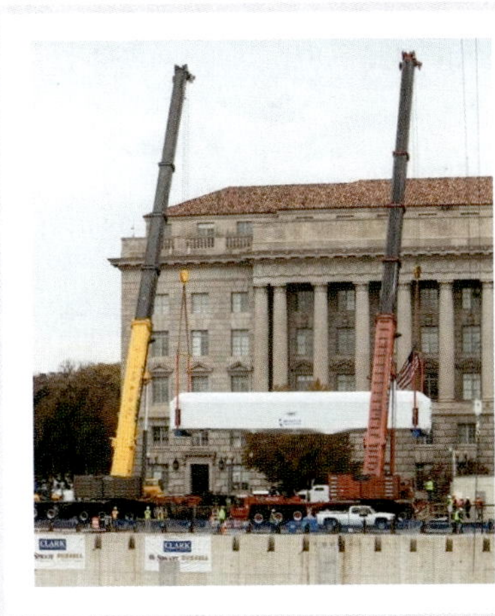

THE MUSEUM BUILT AROUND A TRAIN

There is no easy way to get a railroad car into a building not constructed as a train station. But the genuine segregated Southern Railway car promised to be a worthy addition to the *Defending Freedom, Defining Freedom: Era of Segregation* exhibition. Once the building foundation was secure, Museum officials had the 77-ton carriage hoisted into place by cranes before the walls even went up.

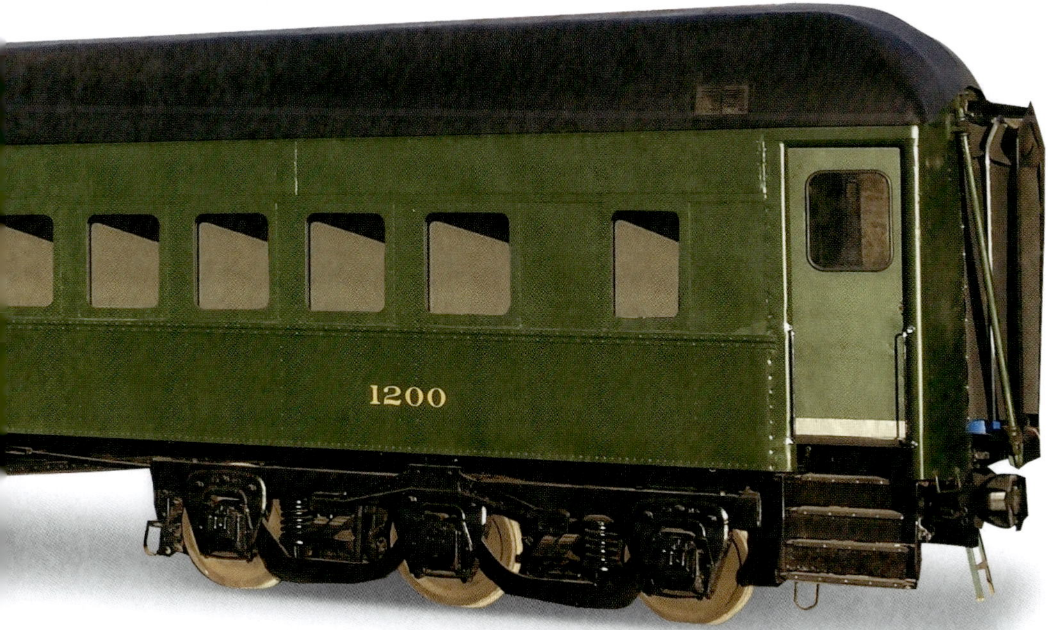

MILITARY

Throughout US history, African Americans have served in the military with the expectation that their sacrifice would earn the right to citizenship and equality for themselves and their community. African Americans hoped that despite the prejudice and discrimination they experienced, their service would contribute to a changed America where racial equality was possible.

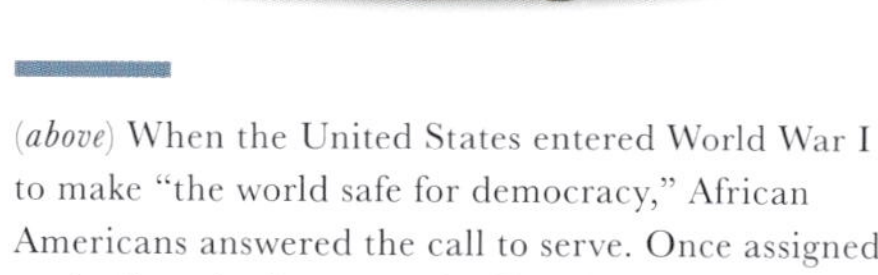

(*above*) When the United States entered World War I to make "the world safe for democracy," African Americans answered the call to serve. Once assigned to the French, they wore the French Adrian helmet.

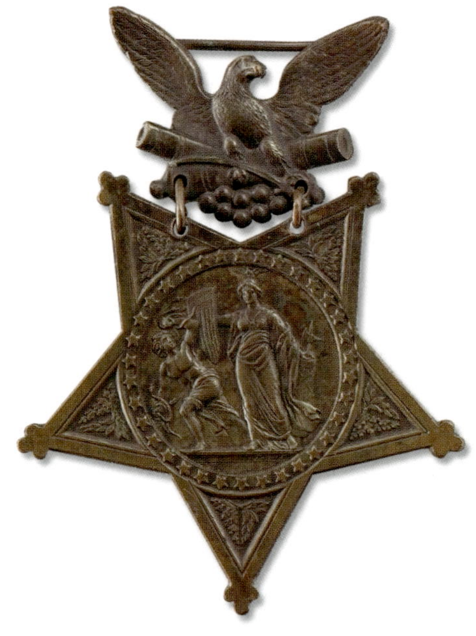

(*above*) Sergeant Thomas Shaw received the Congressional Medal of Honor for his actions at Carrizo Canyon, New Mexico, in 1881. The nation's highest military award was rarely issued to African Americans before the 1990s.

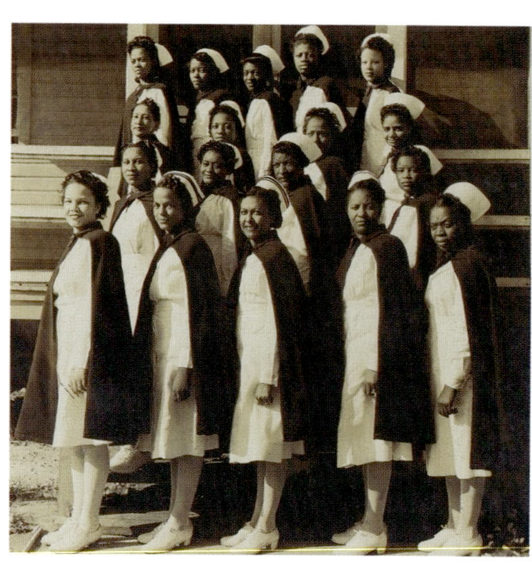

(*right*) African American women have contributed to the military as nurses since the American Revolution. During World War II, Black nurses served throughout the Pacific and in Europe.

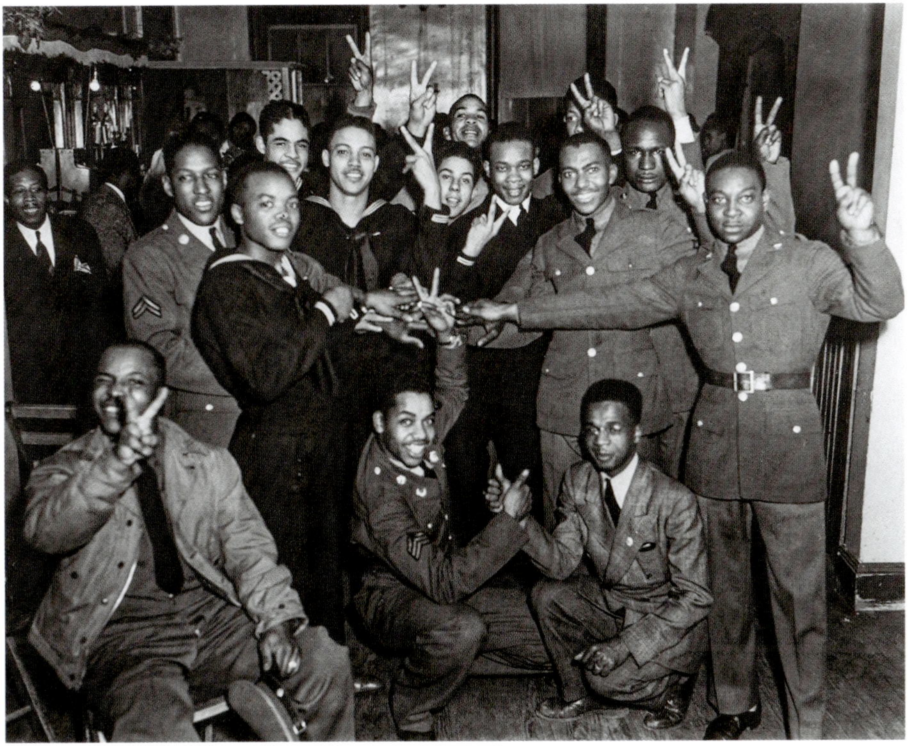

(*above*) One victory down, another still to come: African American servicemen in Brooklyn flash the V for Victory sign in this 1947 photograph by Joe Schwartz.

(*right*) This red, white, and blue handkerchief promoted the Double V campaign: African Americans were fighting for democracy both abroad and on the home front.

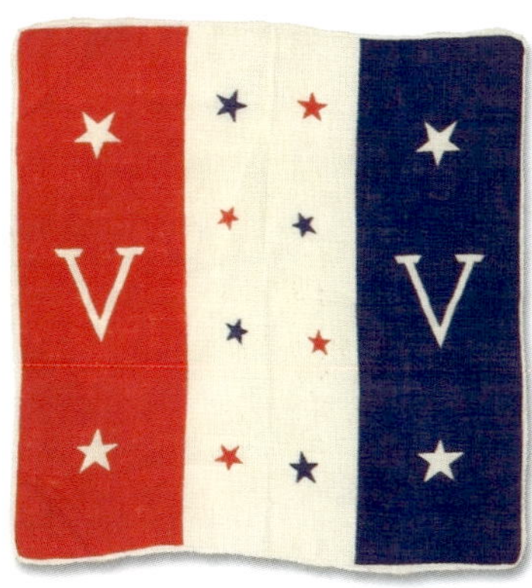

TUSKEGEE AIRMEN

African American fighter pilots known as the Tuskegee Airmen distinguished themselves overseas during World War II, flying thousands of sorties and destroying scores of enemy aircraft, locomotives, and vessels.

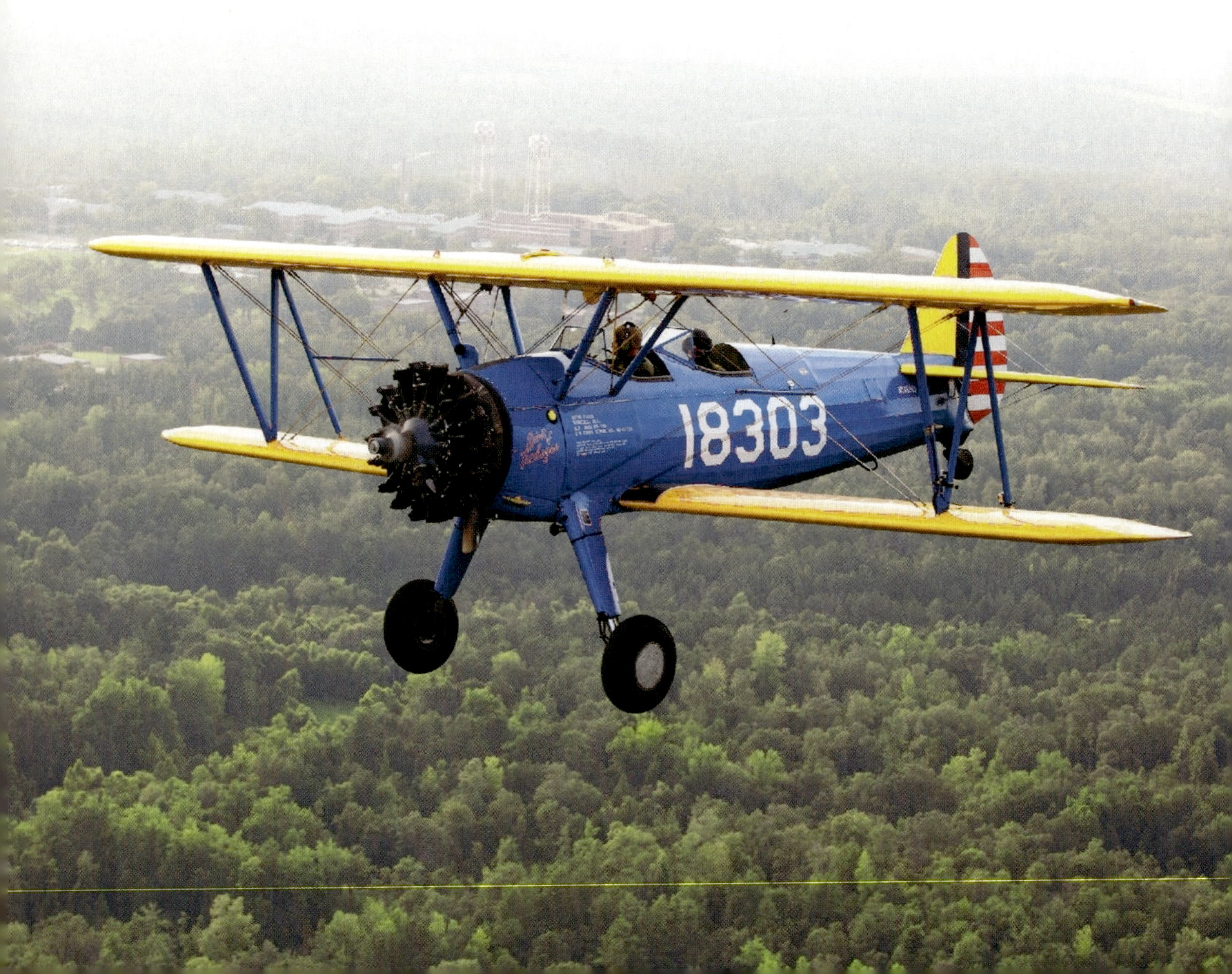

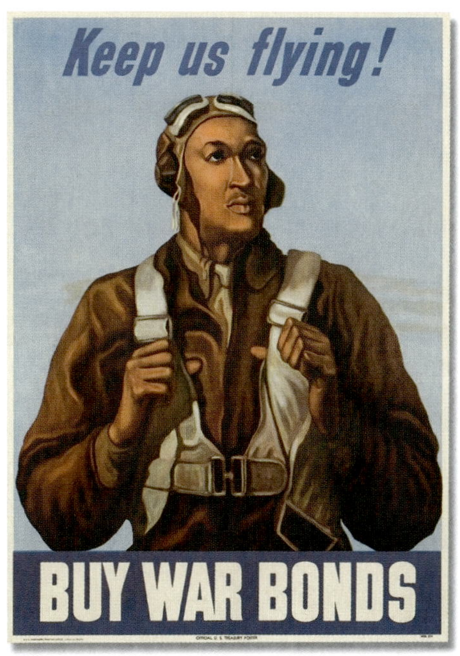

(*above*) A 1943 US Treasury war bonds poster encouraging investment in the war effort featured an image of Tuskegee Airman Robert W. Deiz.

(*above right*) This flight jacket was issued in 1943 to Lt. Col. Woodrow W. Crockett, an original Tuskegee Airman. He subsequently flew 145 combat missions over Italy.

(*left*) A restored airplane, used at Moton Field in Tuskegee, Alabama, to train prospective African American pilots in World War II, takes to the skies again.

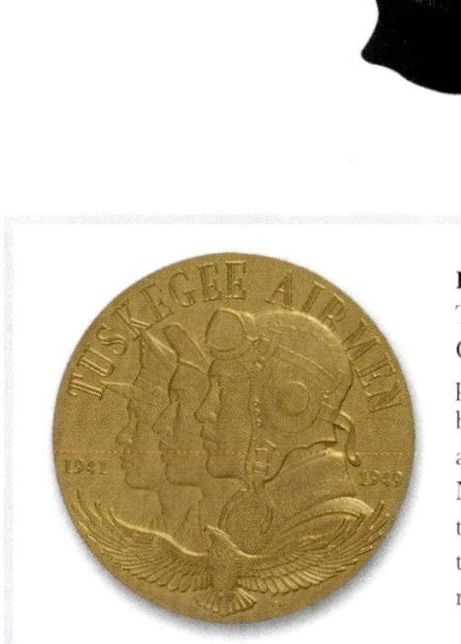

HIGHEST HONOR
The Tuskegee Airmen Congressional Gold Medal, presented to surviving members by President George W. Bush and Speaker of the House Nancy Pelosi in 2007, recognizes their "unique military record that inspired revolutionary reform in the Armed Forces."

THE BLACK PRESS

Since the publication of the first African American newspaper, *Freedom's Journal*, in 1827, African Americans have used the press to establish an independent voice for Black communities and advance the struggle for freedom and equality. Publishers and journalists challenged racism, presented positive images of Black identity, and reflected the cultural breadth of Black people.

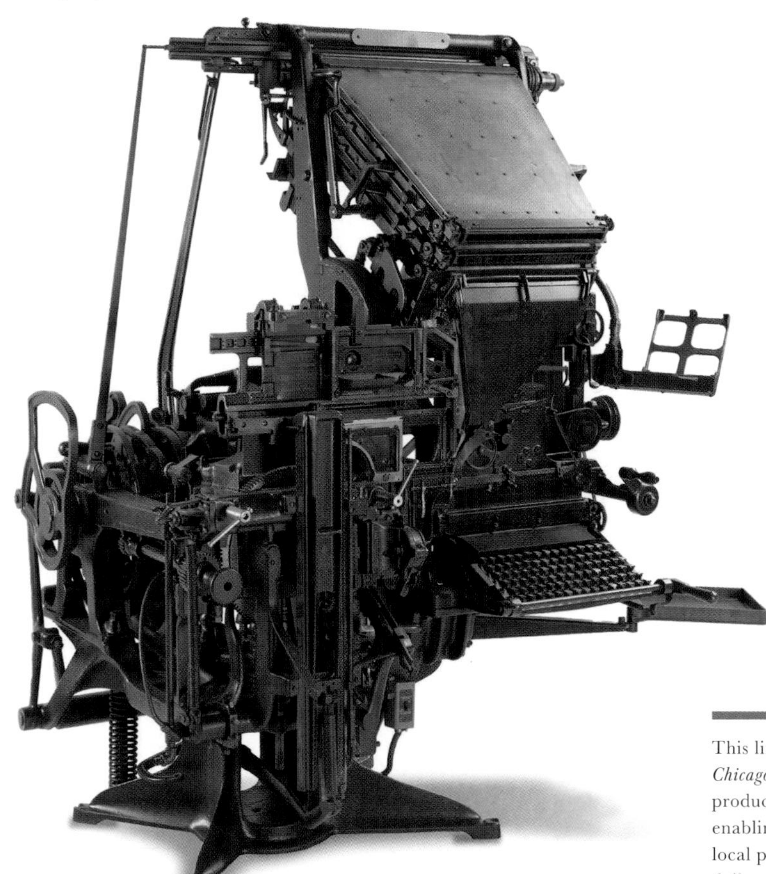

This linotype machine helped the *Chicago Defender* set type rapidly to produce more newspapers faster, enabling it to grow from a small local periodical into a national daily newspaper.

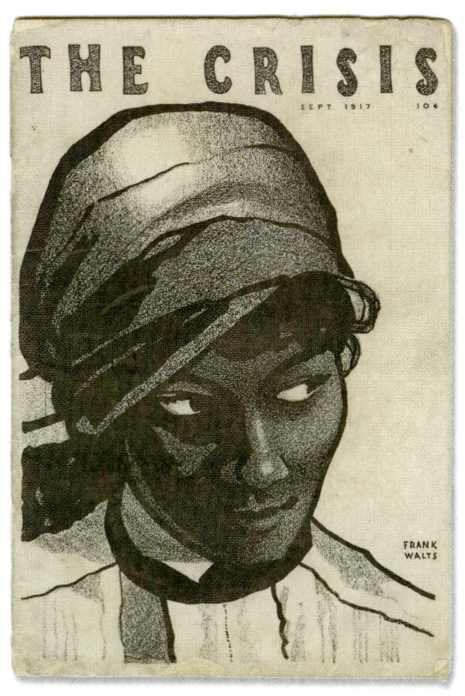

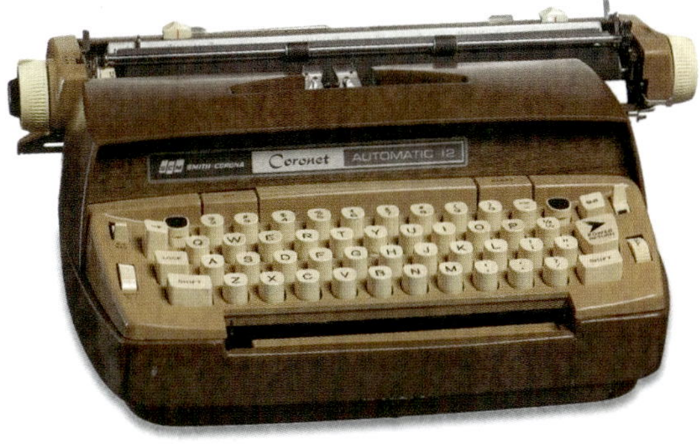

(*above*) W. E. B. Du Bois served as founding editor of *The Crisis*, the official magazine of the National Association for the Advancement of Colored People (NAACP), from 1910 to 1934.

(*above right*) As the first Black reporter at the *Nashville Banner*, Robert Churchwell, who used this typewriter in the 1970s, endured discrimination daily but persevered to support his family, prove his capabilities, and pave the way for other Black journalists.

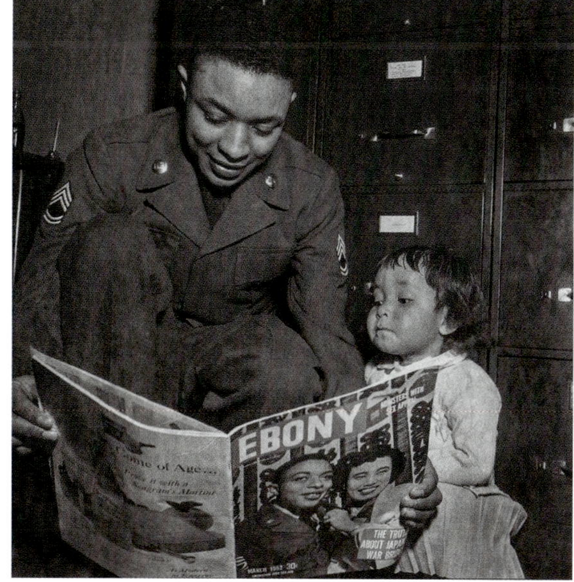

(*right*) Founded in 1945 by John H. Johnson, *Ebony* magazine provided a view of Black America never seen before in popular media.

THE CIVIL RIGHTS MOVEMENT

The 1950s and 1960s, from the Montgomery Bus Boycott to the passing of the Voting Rights Act and beyond, were decades of revolution—years that saw African Americans finally granted the same rights, protections, and privileges that their fellow citizens had long enjoyed.

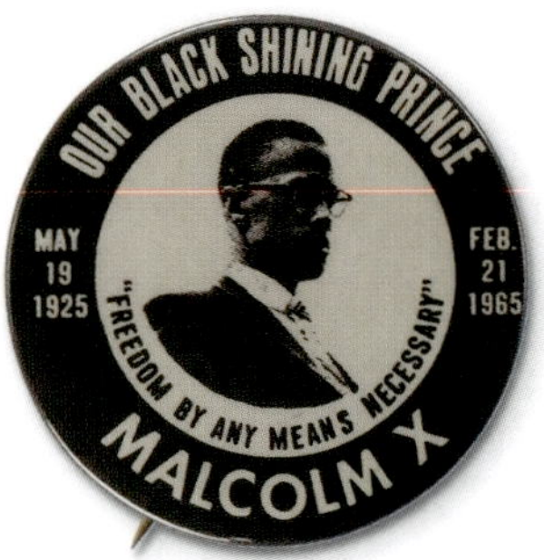

Malcolm X was a prominent leader of the Nation of Islam in the 1950s and early 1960s. This pinback button features his famous saying, "By Any Means Necessary."

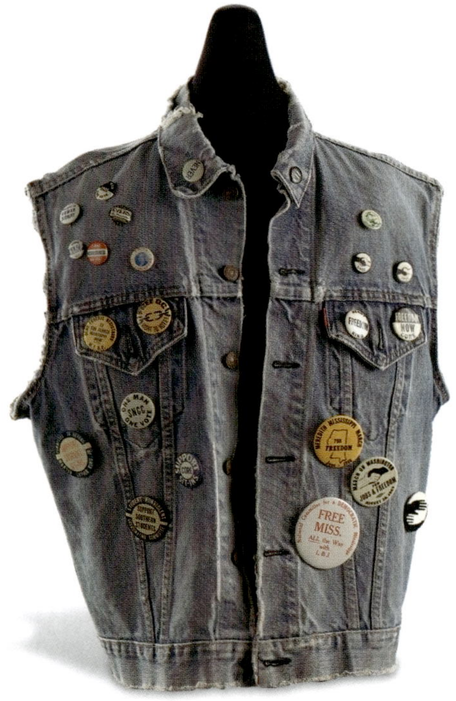

Joan Trumpauer Mulholland assembled the twenty-three pinback buttons pinned across the front of this vest to commemorate her activism during the Civil Rights Movement.

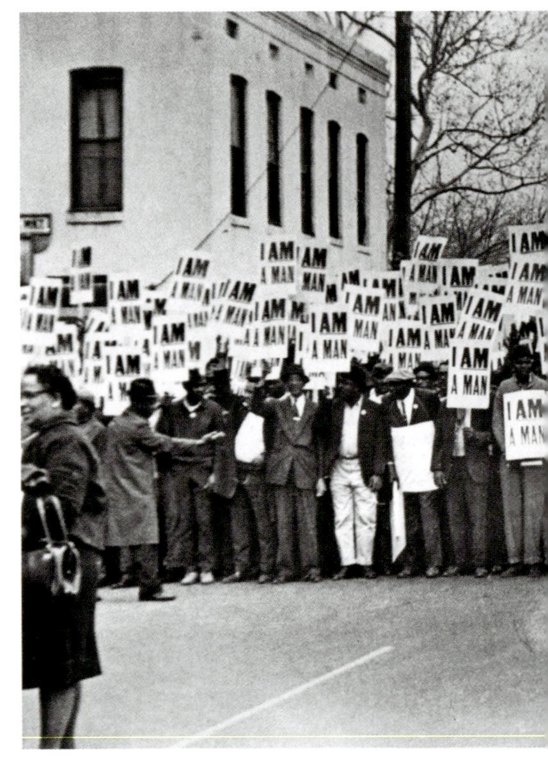

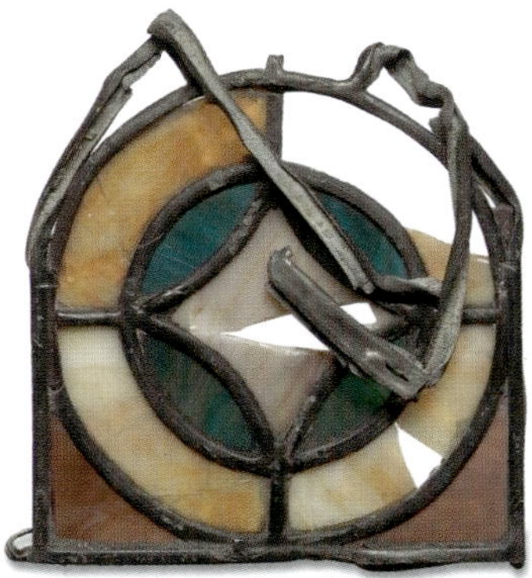

On September 15, 1963, a bomb exploded at the 16th Street Baptist Church in Birmingham, Alabama, killing four children and injuring others. This rosette-shaped shard is from the church's stained glass windows.

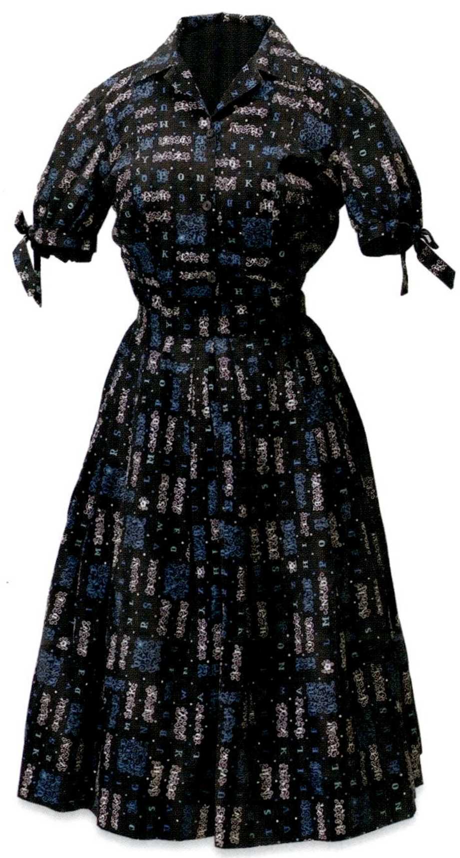

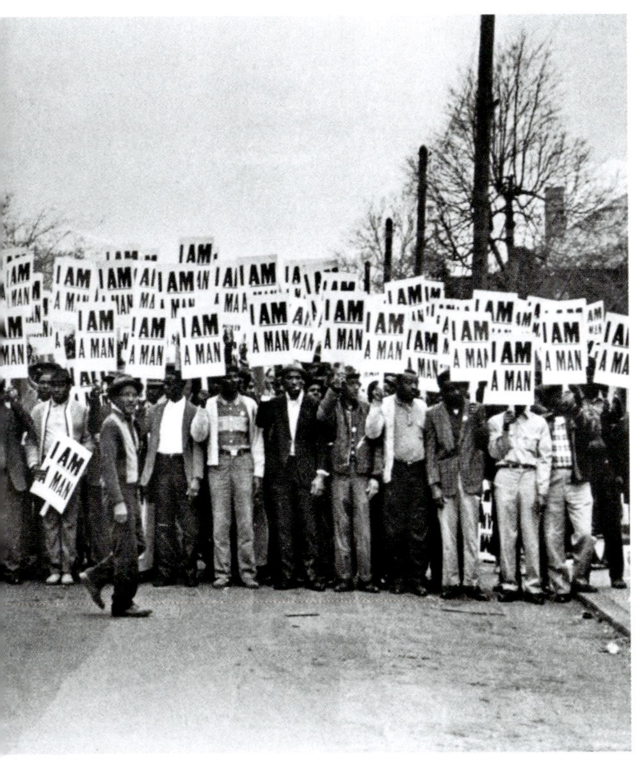

(*above*) One of the Little Rock Nine, Carlotta Walls LaNier wore this outfit on her first day of school as she attempted to integrate Little Rock Central High on September 4, 1957, after the Supreme Court ruling against segregated education.

(*left*) Photojournalist Ernest C. Withers documented these sanitation workers assembled in front of Clayborn Temple for a solidarity march in Memphis, Tennessee, on March 28, 1968.

THE MARCH ON WASHINGTON

In 1963, civil rights leaders A. Philip Randolph and Bayard Rustin began plans for a march in Washington, DC, to protest segregation, voter suppression, and Black unemployment. With support from major civil rights organizations, the August 28 March on Washington for Jobs and Freedom, featuring Dr. Martin Luther King Jr.'s "I Have a Dream" speech, was a resounding success.

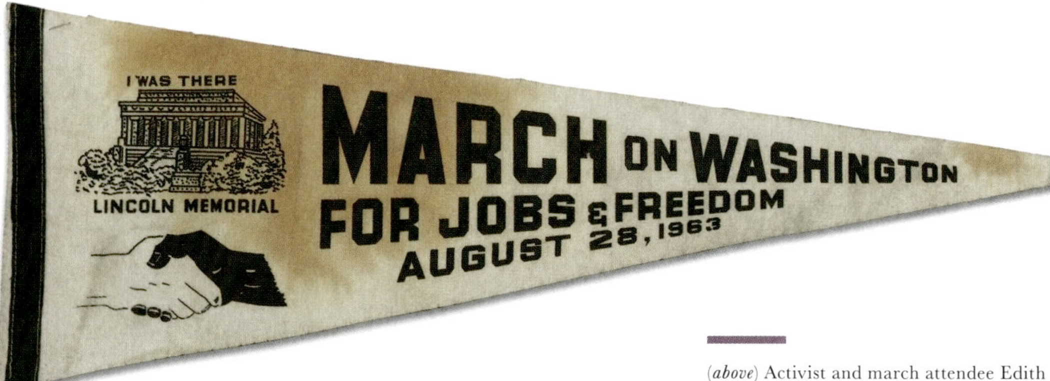

(*above*) Activist and march attendee Edith Lee-Payne carried this souvenir pennant during the March on Washington for Jobs and Freedom.

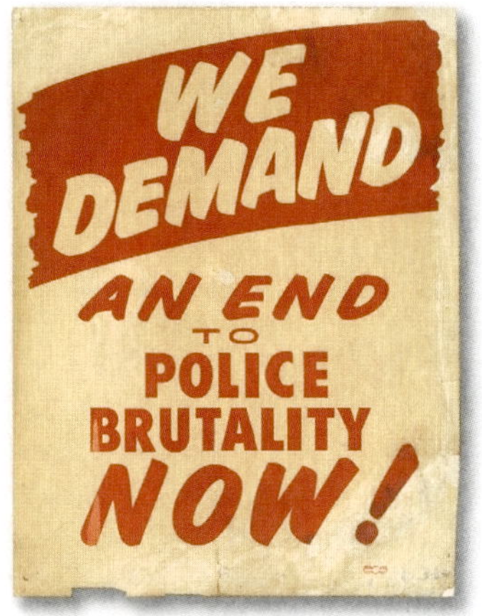

(*left*) This placard declaring "We demand an end to police brutality now!" was used during the March on Washington for Jobs and Freedom.

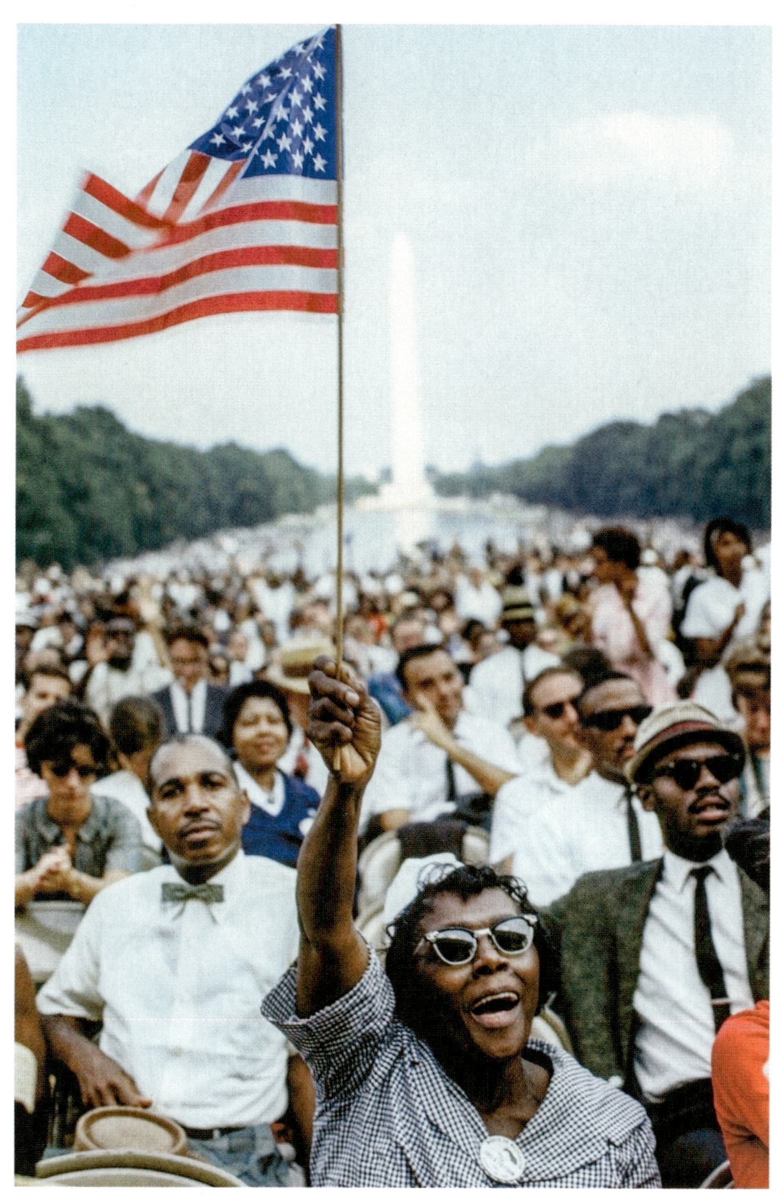

In this photograph of the march by James P. Blair, a large crowd is gathered at the steps of the Lincoln Memorial waiting for Dr. Martin Luther King Jr.'s speech to begin.

BLACK PANTHER PARTY

Founded in 1966 in Oakland, California, the Black Panther Party for Self-Defense was the era's most influential and controversial militant Black Power organization. Its members confronted politicians, challenged the police, and protected Black citizens from brutality. The party produced a variety of community service programs while its leaders advocated for social and cultural revolution.

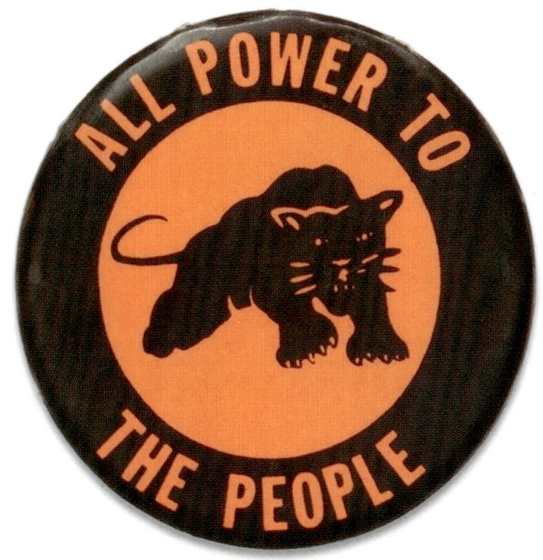

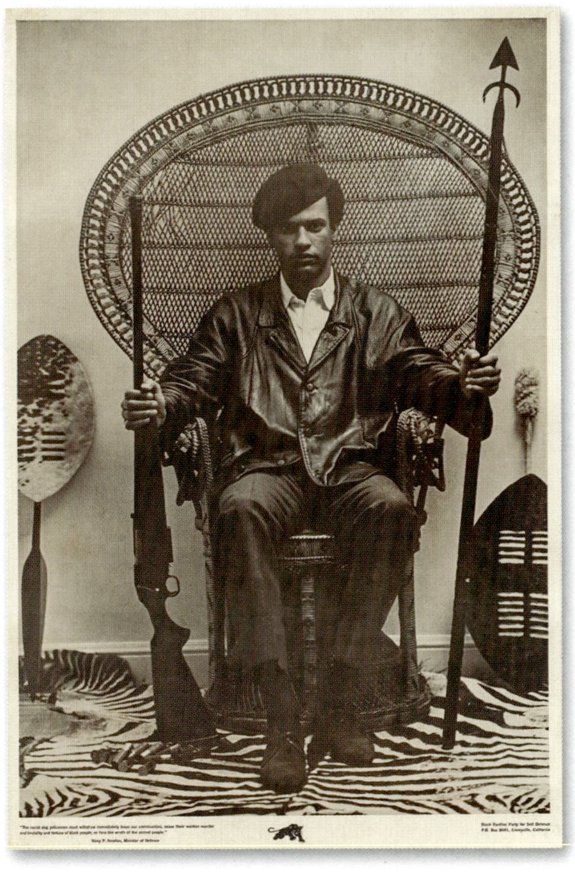

(*above*) This Black Panther Party pinback button features the party's logo and mantra, "All power to the people."

(*right*) Combining African imagery with symbols of armed struggle, this poster depicting party cofounder Huey Newton was included in the initial publication of the Panthers' Ten Point Program for social change.

SHIRLEY CHISHOLM

Shirley Chisholm was the first African American woman elected to Congress and the first to campaign for the presidency. The daughter of immigrants, the Brooklyn-born congresswoman campaigned against Hubert Humphrey and George McGovern for the Democratic Party nomination for president and advocated for social and economic equality for all Americans.

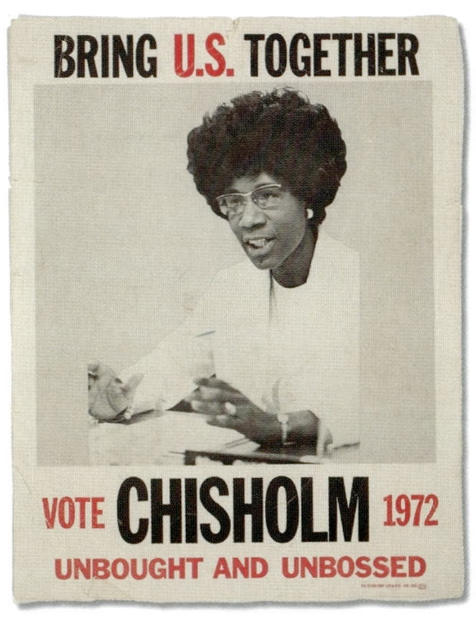

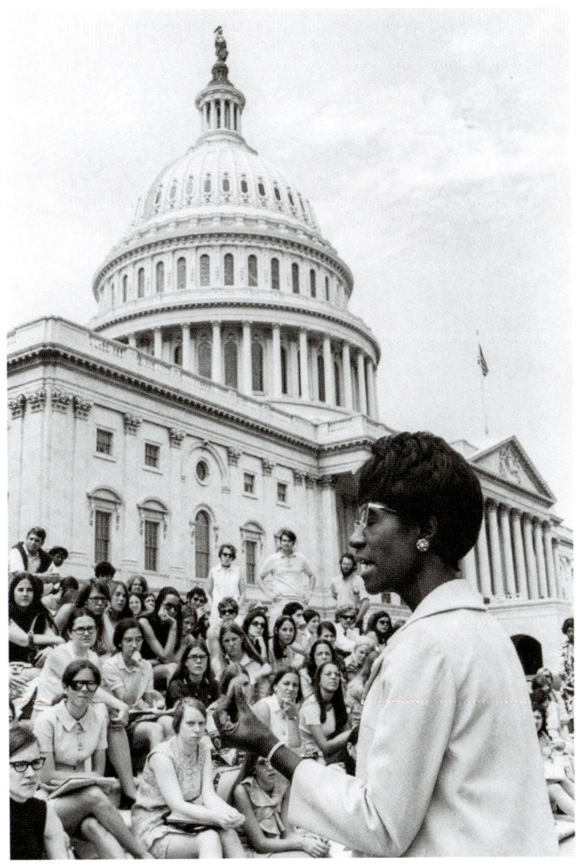

(*left*) Photographer Maurice Sorrell captured this image of Chisholm addressing a group of students in front of the United States Capitol.

(*above*) Congresswoman Chisholm chose the campaign slogan "Unbought and Unbossed" for her 1972 presidential bid.

TWENTY-FIRST-CENTURY ACTIVISM

The present-day activism of African Americans has built upon the legacy of the Civil Rights and Black Power Movements of the twentieth century. Focused on systemic change and galvanized primarily through the internet and social media, twenty-first-century African American activism is characterized through a wide range of organizations, movements, and ideologies that challenge inequality across various spheres of life.

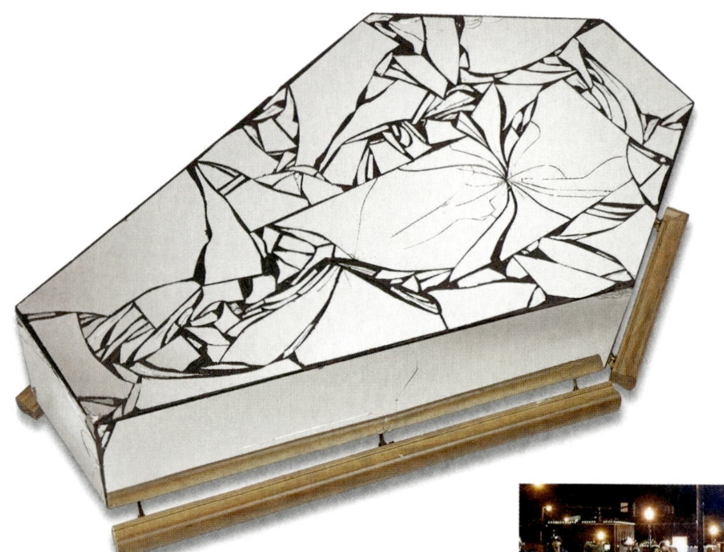

(*left*) Creating art to express a community's collective anguish over the killing of Michael Brown Jr., local artists designed the *Mirror Casket* sculpture and used other forms of protest art during the Ferguson, Missouri, unrest of 2014.

(*below*) The *Mirror Casket* being carried during a protest march for Black lives in Ferguson in 2014. This photograph is from Zun Lee's *Black Love Matters* series.

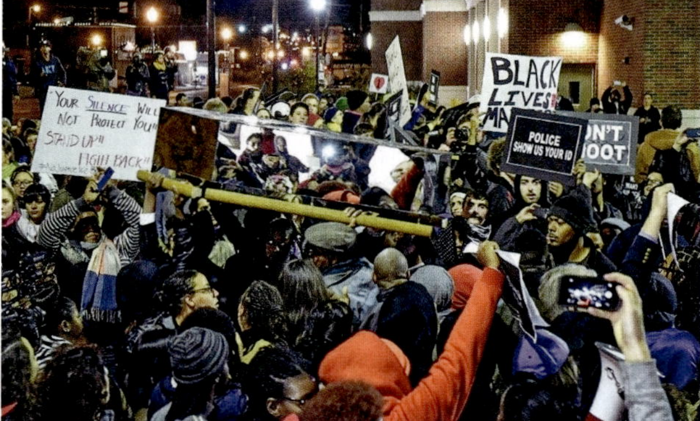

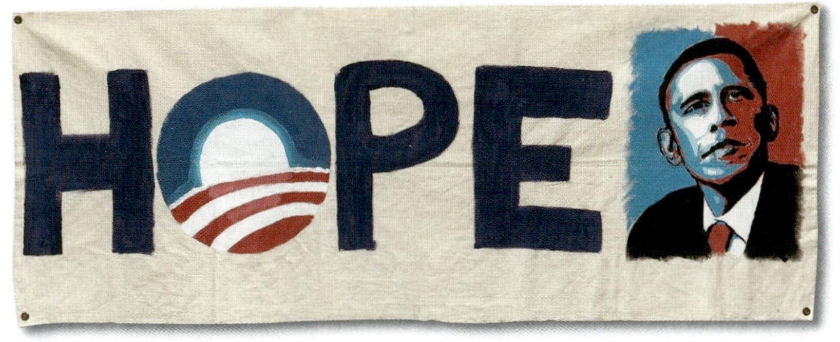

This hand-painted campaign banner from Columbia, Missouri, features a rendition of the Shepard Fairey portrait of Barack Obama and the 2008 campaign slogan.

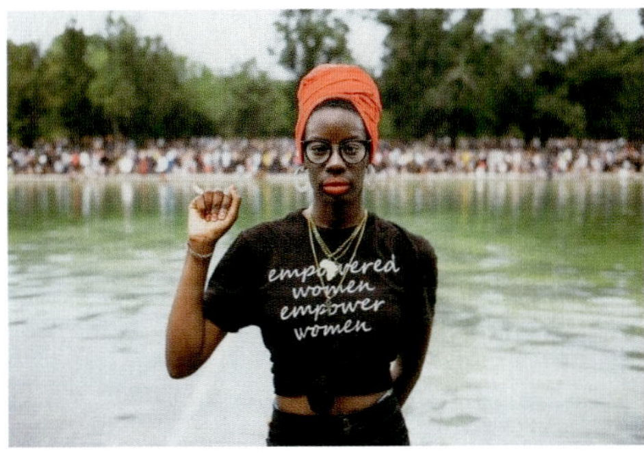

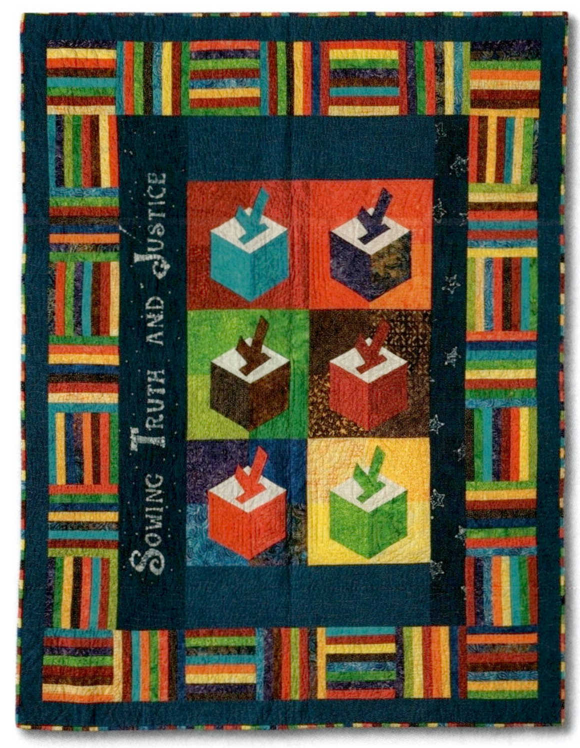

(*above*) This image by photographer Tony Mobley titled *Empowered* depicts Kheeda "Key" Cruickshank with her right fist raised up during the 2020 social justice protests in Washington, DC.

(*right*) This quilt by the Sowing Truth and Justice Collective commemorates the 2018 founding of Fair Fight Action, an organization combating voter suppression led by Georgia politician Stacey Abrams.

SPORTS

Even when integration was still unthinkable, sports gave African Americans the chance to beat bigotry and discrimination. Black heroes emerged from boxing, football, and other sporting arenas, winning races, throwing punches, and making touchdowns that gave Black people increased hope and self-worth—and role models they could emulate.

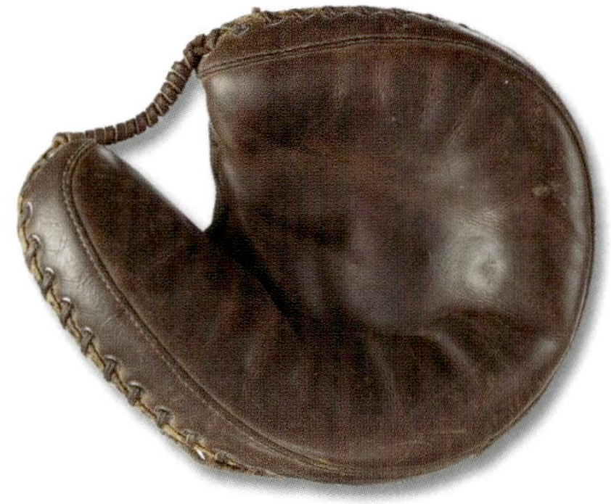

(*above*) Roy Campanella was the first African American catcher in Major League Baseball, and a three-time National League MVP. He wore this mitt during his career with the Brooklyn Dodgers.

(*right*) This was the official program for the 1973 fight between two undefeated heavyweights, Joe Frazier and George Foreman. Foreman dominated the fight held in Kingston, Jamaica, securing the title of heavyweight champion.

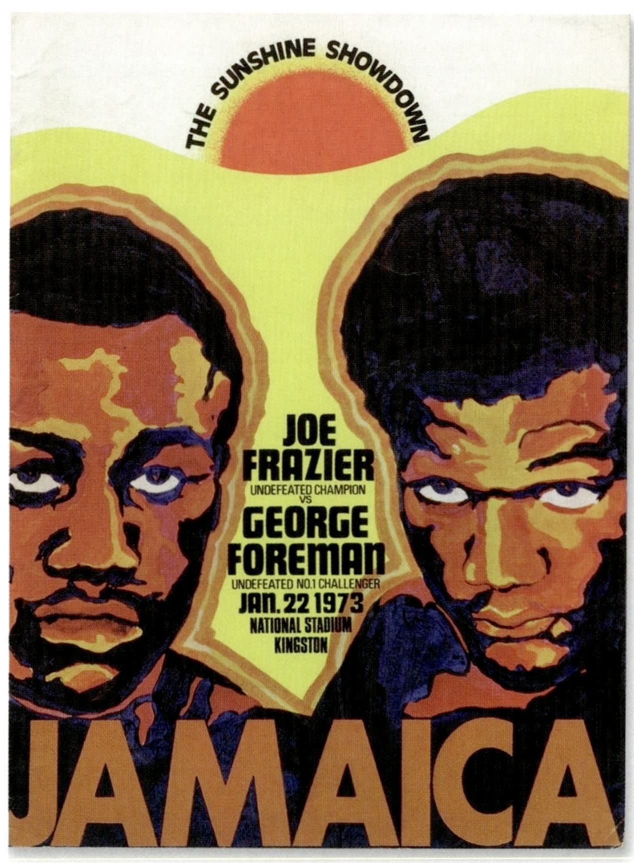

(*right*) Figure skater Debi Thomas wore this costume when she won the US and World Championships in 1986. In 1988, Thomas became the first African American to win a medal at the Winter Olympic Games.

(*below*) Founded in 1978 by coach Neal Henderson, the Fort Dupont Ice Hockey Club in Southeast Washington, DC, is the nation's oldest minority youth hockey program.

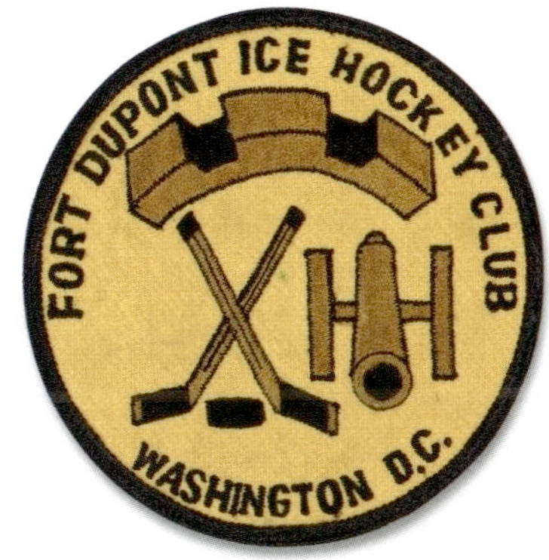

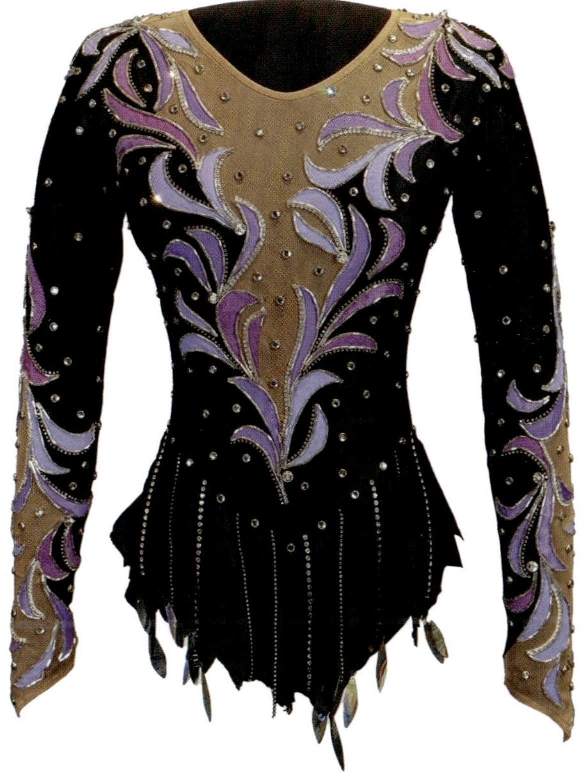

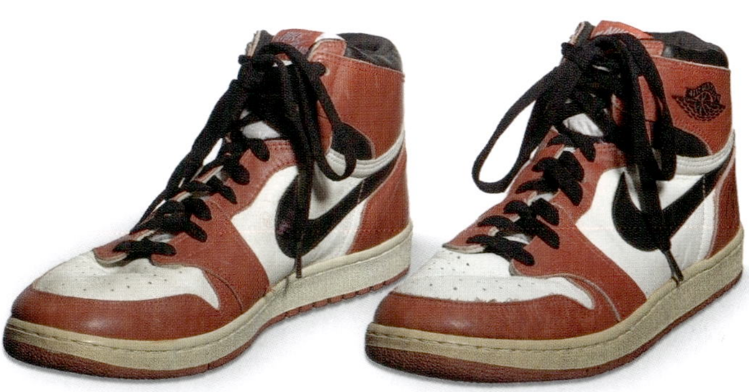

Legendary basketball player Michael Jordan helped transform the National Basketball Association in the 1980s through his exciting, skilled style of play and the launch of the Nike Air Jordan sneaker line in 1984.

OLYMPICS

Since the first modern Olympics in 1896, the Olympic Games have been an international stage to demonstrate superior athletic ability and display exemplary character and conduct. As African Americans fought prejudice at home, the Olympics provided an opportunity for them to disrupt negative stereotypes and show their athletic discipline and intellectual capacity—before a worldwide audience.

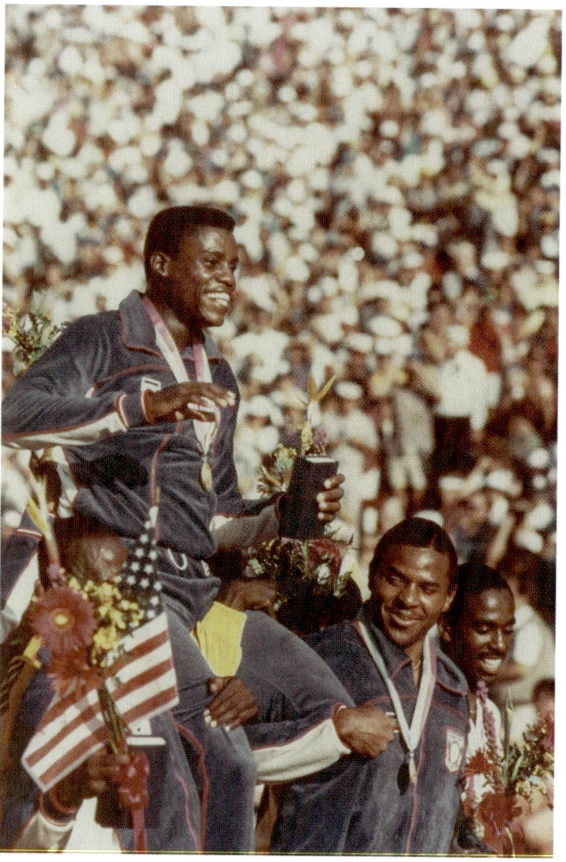

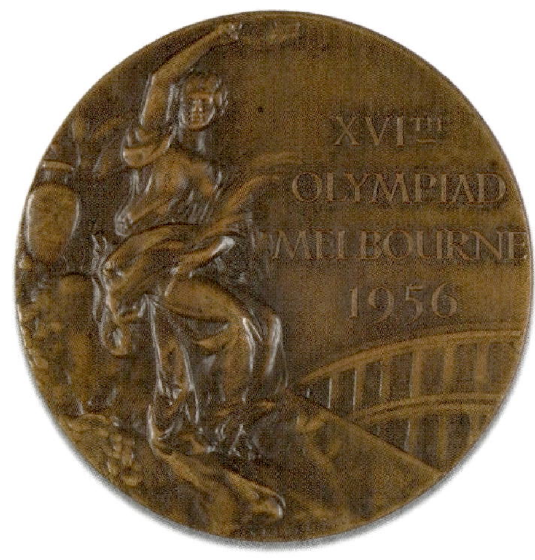

(*left*) Carl Lewis, winner of ten Olympic medals, is seen here after winning his fourth gold medal at the 1987 Olympic Games in Los Angeles.

(*above*) Claiming bronze at the 1956 Melbourne Olympics, Isabelle Daniels, whose medal is seen here, joined Wilma Rudolph, Mae Faggs, and Margaret Matthews in becoming the first all–African American women's relay team to win an Olympic medal.

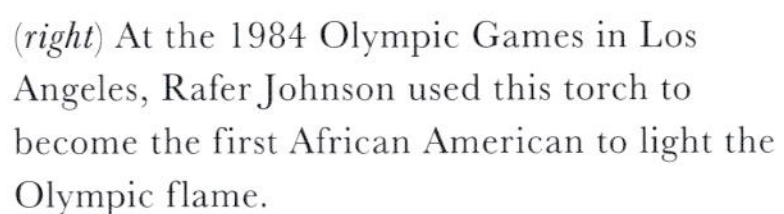

(*right*) At the 1984 Olympic Games in Los Angeles, Rafer Johnson used this torch to become the first African American to light the Olympic flame.

(*below*) This enamel US Olympics flag pin was owned by Jesse Owens, a four-time gold medal winner at the 1936 Berlin Olympics.

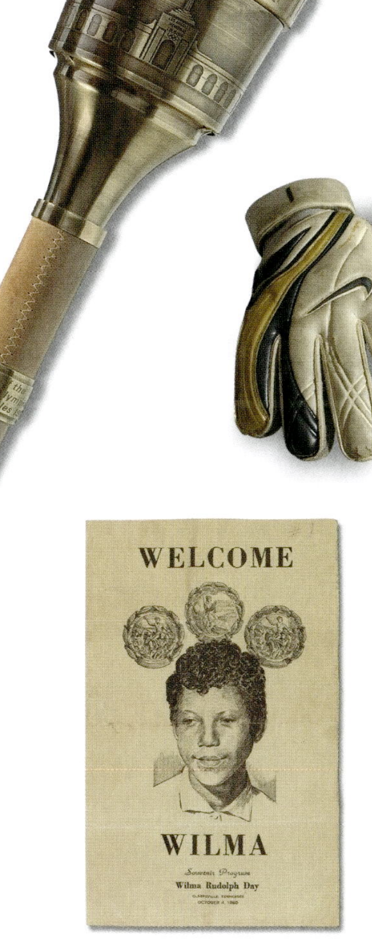

(*above*) Briana Scurry, the only African American woman goalkeeper in Team USA women's soccer history, wore these goalie gloves as part of the gold medal–winning team at the 2004 Athens Olympics.

(*left*) Sprinter Wilma Rudolph won three gold medals at the 1960 Rome Olympics. Wilma Rudolph Day, a celebration in her hometown of Clarksville, Tennessee, was the first integrated public event in the city.

CULTURAL EXPRESSIONS

Held within and passed through families and communities, culture reflects beliefs, informs behavior, fosters creativity, and, most of all, sustains the spirit during times of overwhelming adversity. This creativity is everywhere in the day-to-day lives of African Americans. It is in the food eaten, languages spoken, art created, and many other forms of cultural expression.

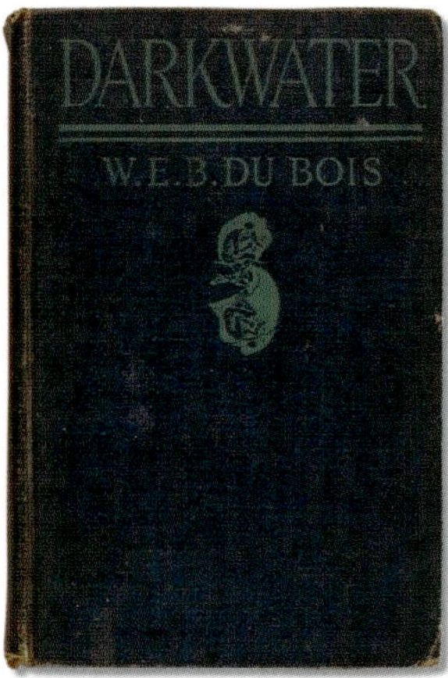

Published in 1920, *Darkwater* is the first in a trilogy of autobiographies by sociologist, historian, and activist W. E. B. Du Bois. The book incorporates essays, spirituals, and poems along with traditional autobiographical stories.

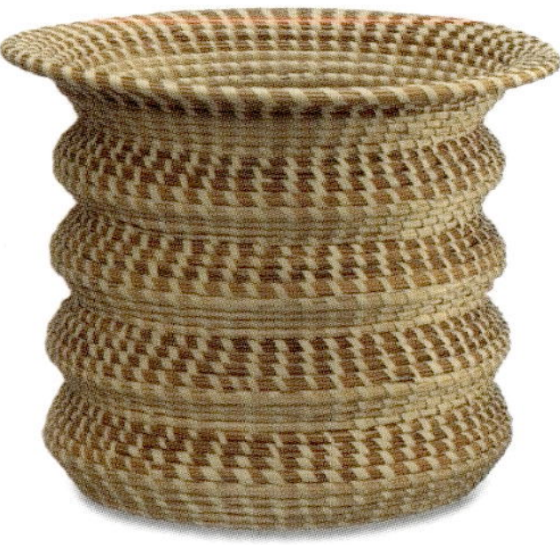

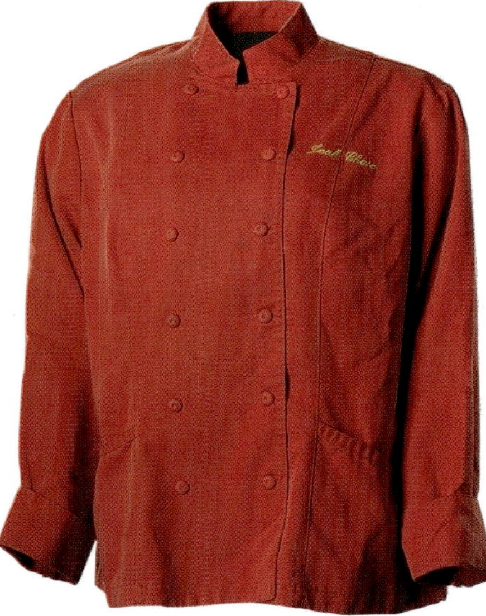

(*above*) Sweetgrass baskets originated in rice-growing areas on the West African coast. South Carolina artisan Mary Jackson learned the craft from her family and now develops new designs like this one using traditional materials.

(*left*) Chef Leah Chase brought New Orleans Creole cooking to international attention. Her restaurant, Dooky Chase's, was a gathering place for civil rights organizers in the 1950s.

DESIGN

Design shapes the world around us through innovation, function, and creative expression. The impact of African Americans in design is reflected in American material culture and the built environment we experience today.

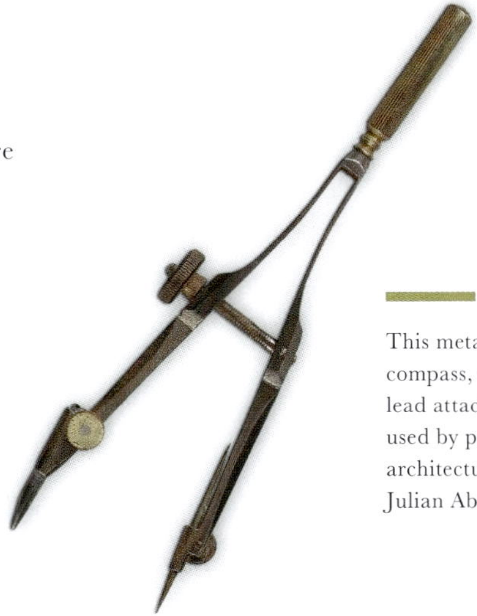

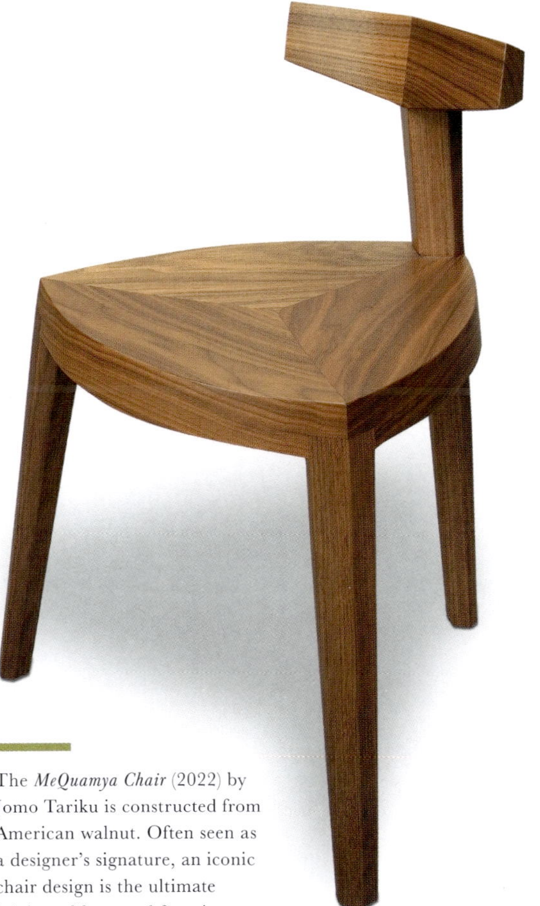

The *MeQuamya Chair* (2022) by Jomo Tariku is constructed from American walnut. Often seen as a designer's signature, an iconic chair design is the ultimate joining of form and function.

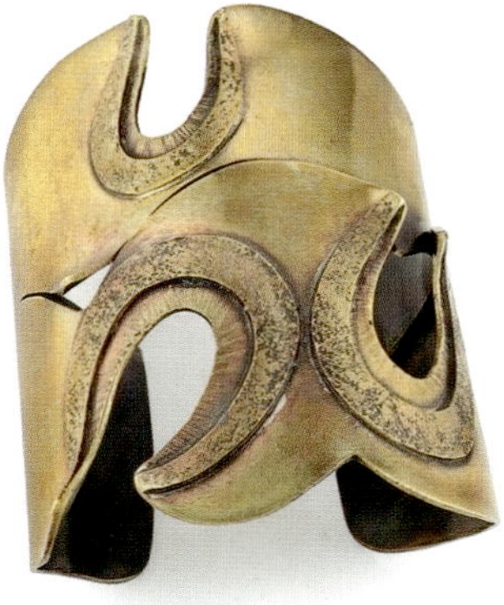

This metal drawing compass, with lead attached, was used by prominent architectural engineer Julian Abele Cook Sr.

Art Smith was a significant figure in the mid-century modernist jewelry movement. He used his training as a sculptor to create a "wearable art" style of jewelry such as this *Three Hole* cuff.

A TRADITION OF QUILTING

Many patches make masterpieces: African Americans have transformed quilting from a labor of dire necessity—using scraps of fabric, worn-out clothing, even empty feed sacks—into an abstract and improvisational art with great storytelling power.

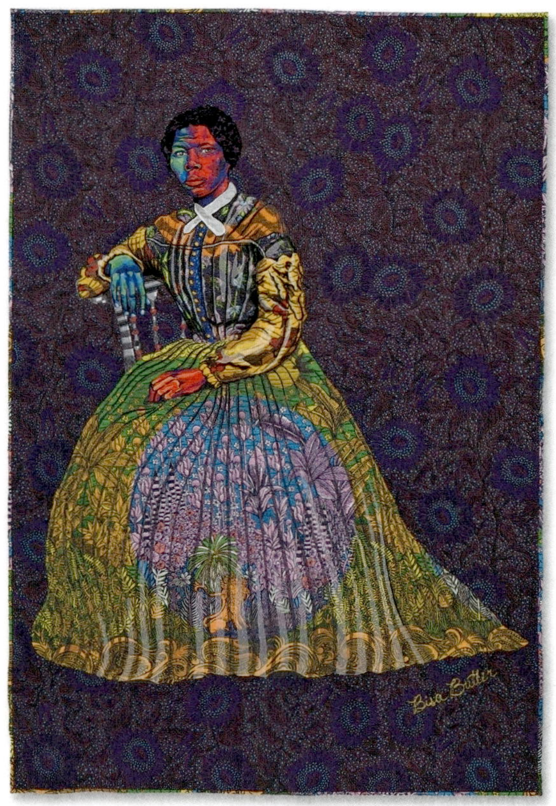

(*left*) In *I Go To Prepare A Place For You* (2021), fiber artist Bisa Butler used African-based fabrics in symbolic colors, textures, and patterns to create a quilted portrait of Harriet Tubman based on the earliest known photograph of her (see p. 14).

(*below*) *Silo*, a strip-style quilt made in 2007 by Mensie Lee Pettway of Gee's Bend, Alabama, reflects the quilting traditions of three generations of her family.

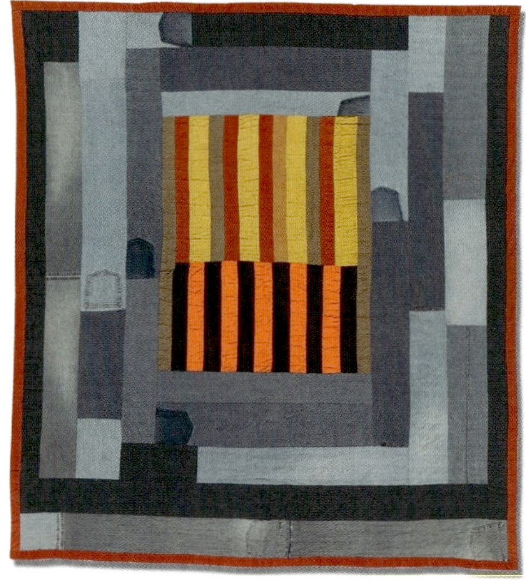

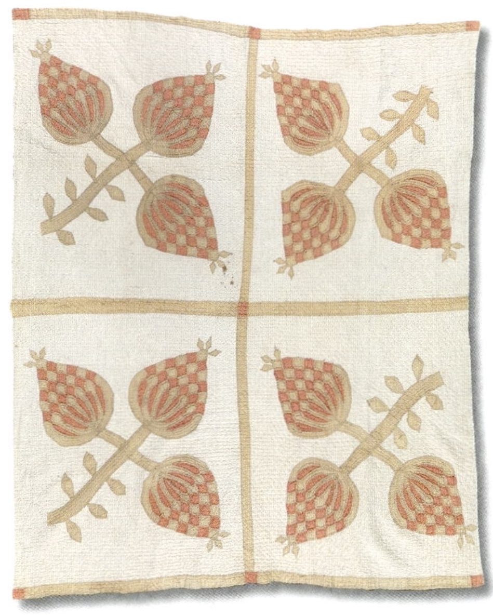

This quilt with a pineapple motif, symbolizing home and family, was made by Lydia Hardiman in Lyles Station, Indiana, in 1885, as a wedding gift for her daughter Lucy Hardiman Roundtree.

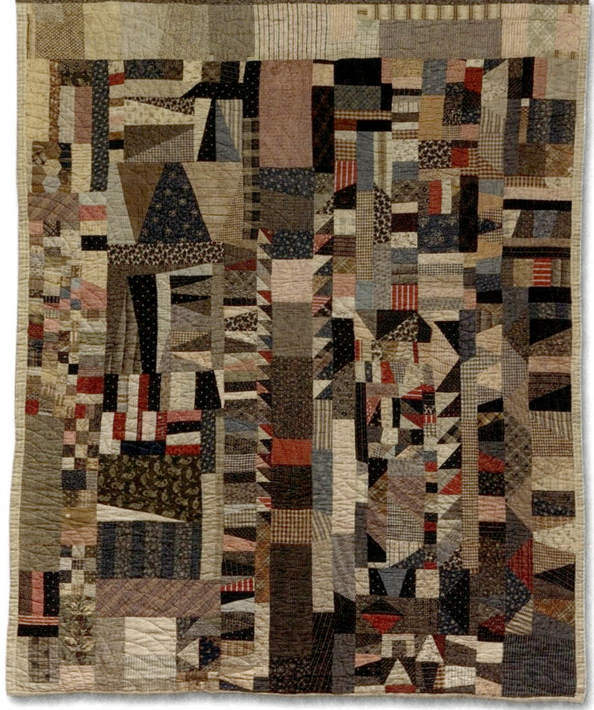

This quilt was made by Elizabeth Salter Smith, a formerly enslaved woman in Georgia, in the late nineteenth century from fabric scraps cut into an array of geometric shapes.

MAE REEVES

One of the first African American female business owners in downtown Philadelphia, Mae Reeves provided her clients with an essential item of fashion in the 1940s and 1950s: a hat. Ella Fitzgerald, Lena Horne, and Marian Anderson all purchased hats from Mae's Millinery Shop.

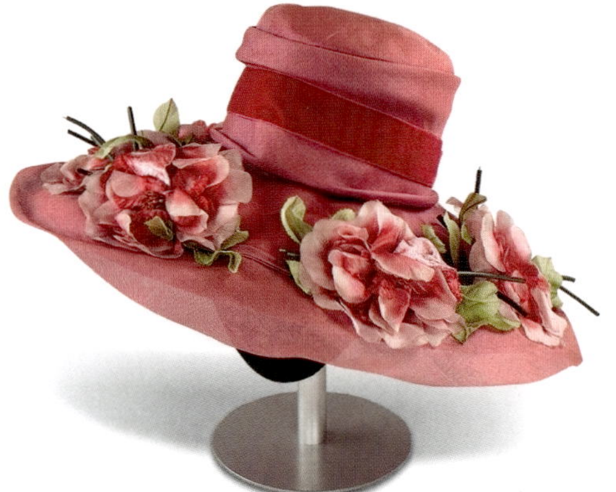

(*left*) A wide-brimmed hat adorned with pink flowers from Mae's Millinery Shop.

(*right*) A turban made by Reeves in rust satin and black lace.

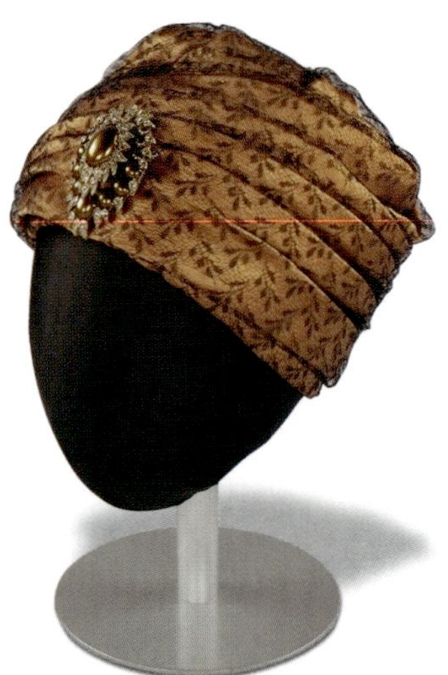

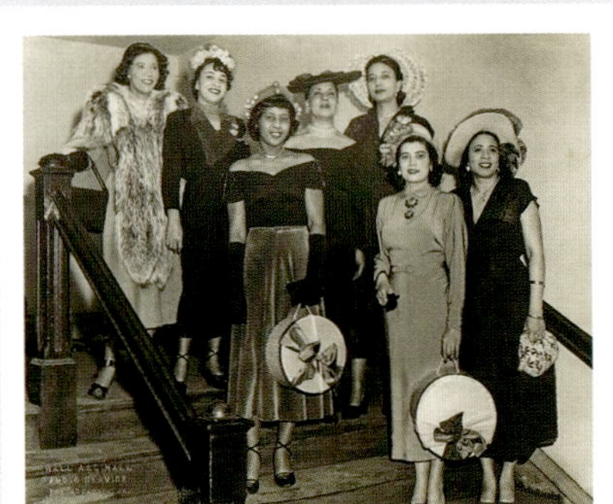

PROPER TOPPER In a photograph taken around 1950, Mae Reeves stands on the bottom step on the right—in a white hat—with hat-wearing companions.

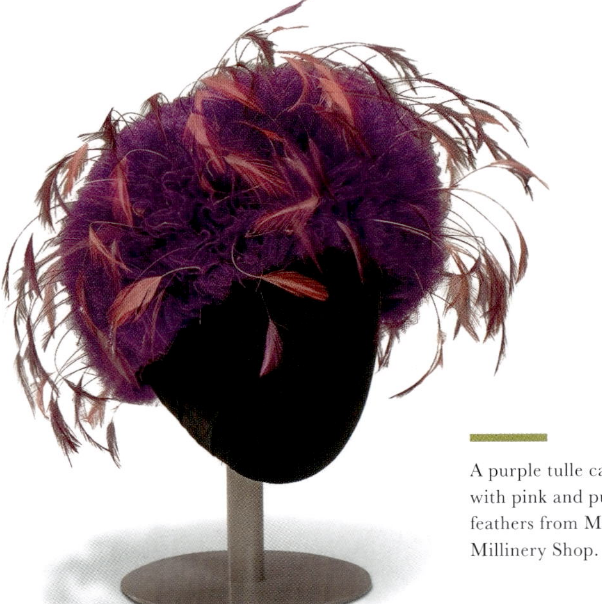

A purple tulle cap with pink and purple feathers from Mae's Millinery Shop.

ANN LOWE

Many a socialite visited Ann Lowe's Gowns, a salon on Manhattan's Lexington Avenue, in the 1950s. The daughter and granddaughter of African American seamstresses, Lowe designed the wedding dress worn by Jacqueline Bouvier when she married John F. Kennedy in 1953.

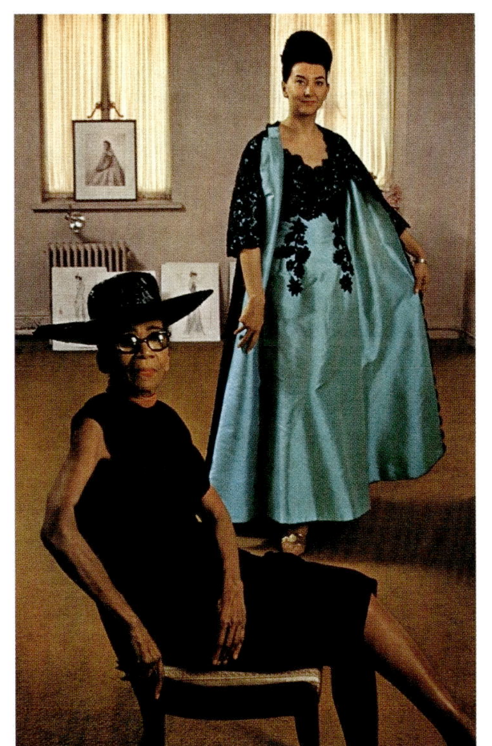

SOCIETY'S BEST KEPT SECRET Ann Lowe in her New York City salon in 1966 with model Judith Palmer wearing a Lowe-designed theater gown and coat.

Designed in 1966, this dress is referred to as the "American Beauty Ball Gown," for the variety of roses adorning the back and shoulders.

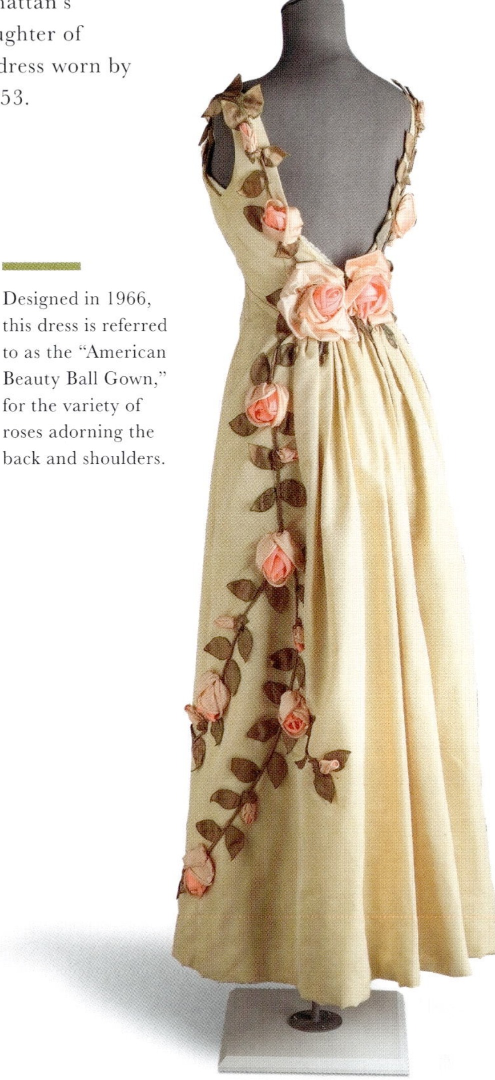

MUSICAL CROSSROADS

African American music has influenced nearly all aspects of the American musical landscape, transforming American music into a unique blend of traditions. As a vibrant, living art, music is a vehicle of cultural expression, granting a voice to the emotions and shared humanity of all people.

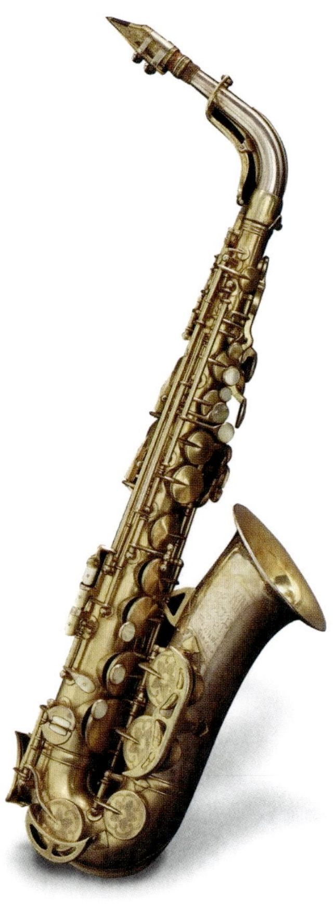

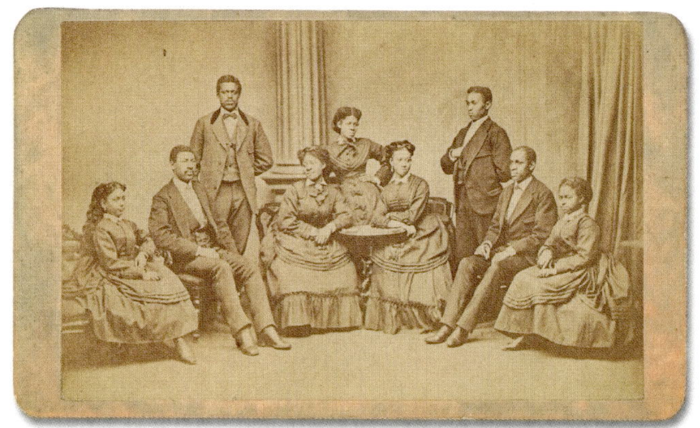

(*left*) This alto saxophone was owned and played by musical pioneer and jazz virtuoso Charlie Parker.

(*above*) In 1871, the Fisk Jubilee Singers embarked on a fundraising tour for Fisk University that brought spiritual music onto the concert stage, introducing it to an international audience.

(*right*) One of the original gospel crossover artists, Sister Rosetta Tharpe sang and played electric guitar in both sacred and secular venues.

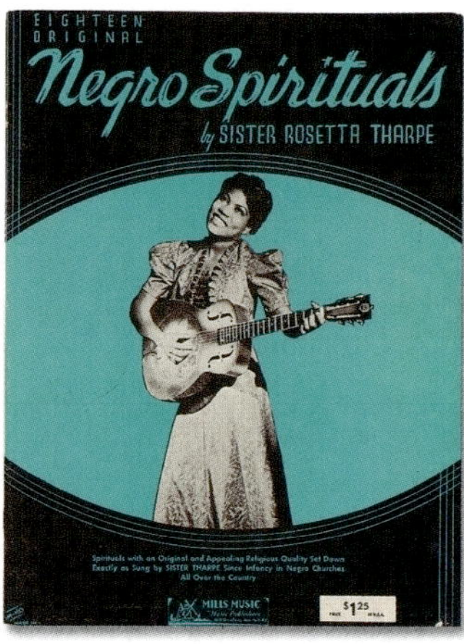

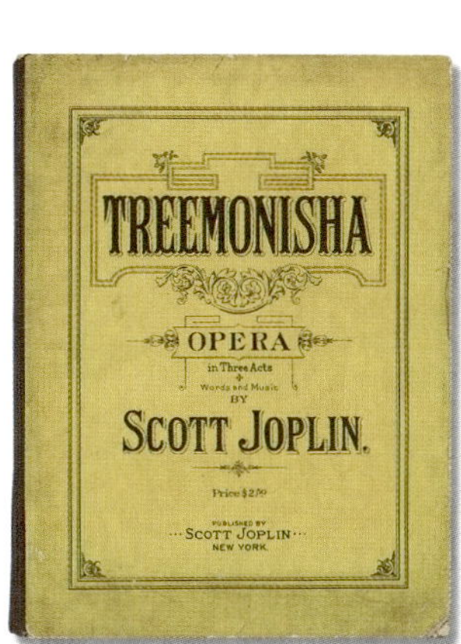

A black-and-yellow music score for *Treemonisha: Opera in Three Acts* (1911), written and published by ragtime composer Scott Joplin.

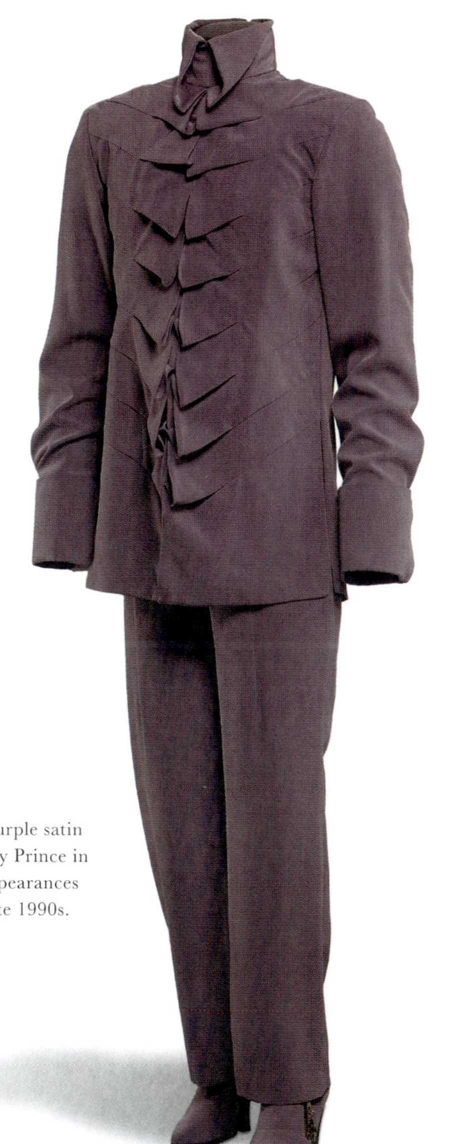

A lavender purple satin outfit worn by Prince in numerous appearances during the late 1990s.

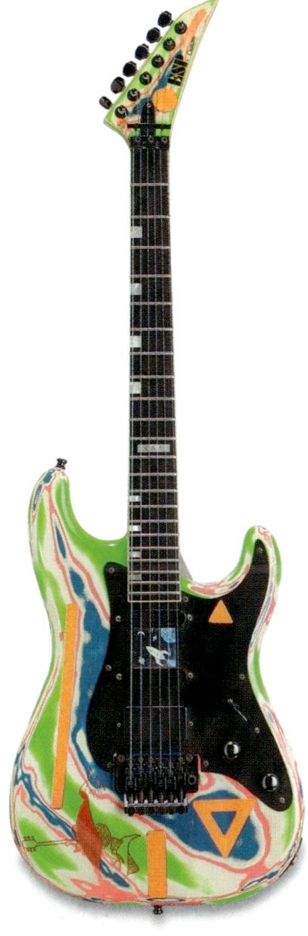

Vernon Reid of the band Living Colour used this multicolored custom designed guitar to record their smash hit "Cult of Personality" from their debut album *Vivid* (1988).

MUSIC POSTERS

Since the music industry's earliest days, posters, photographs, and other graphic images have been used to advertise and promote artists and their performances. Before the digital age, cardboard posters and paper leaflets helped spread the word of musicians touring and making stops through different towns and cities.

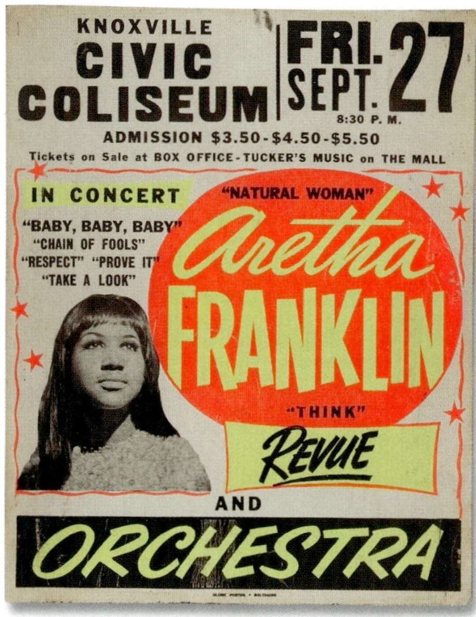

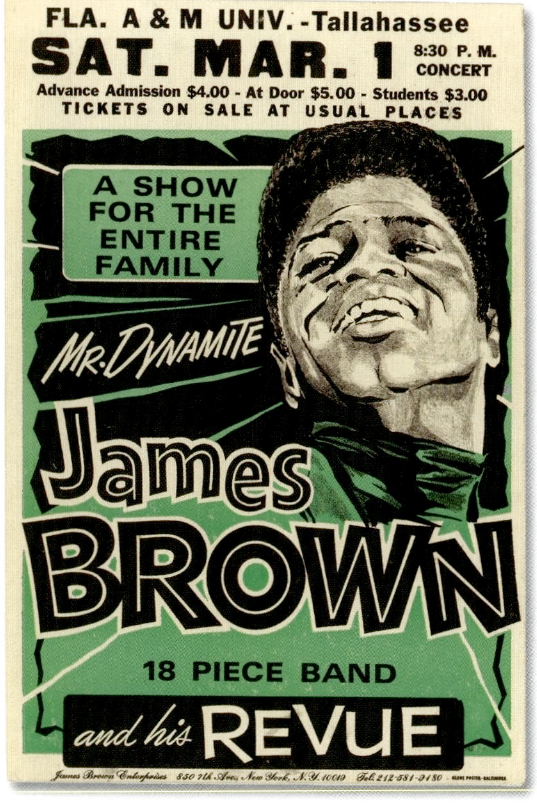

(*left*) The Globe Poster Printing Company of Baltimore, Maryland, created this eye-catching poster in 1969 to entice families to attend a James Brown concert at Florida A&M University.

(*above*) This Globe poster advertising Aretha Franklin's 1968 performance at the Knoxville Civic Coliseum in Tennessee is outlined in red with graphic stars highlighting the titles of her hit songs.

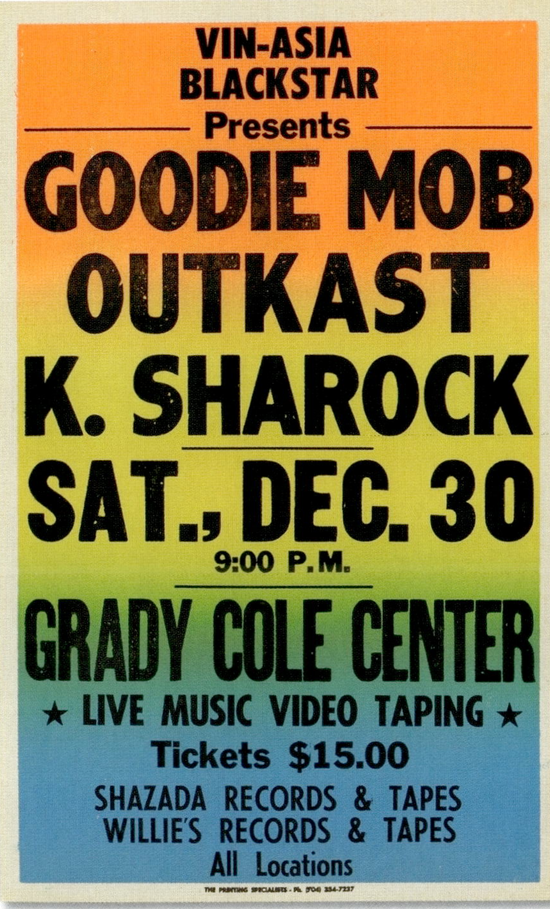

(*left*) Concert poster advertising a 1995 show featuring Goodie Mob, Outkast, and K. Sharock at the Grady Cole Center in Charlotte, North Carolina.

(*below*) This colorful poster shows scenes from *Space Is the Place*, the 1974 Afrofuturist science-fiction film conceived, cowritten, and starring Sun Ra and his Arkestra.

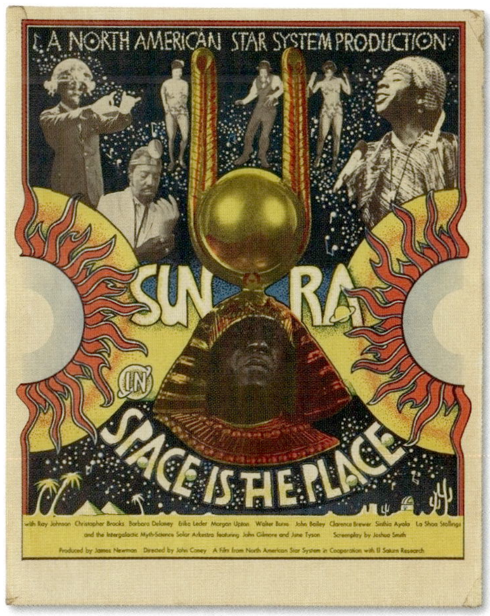

POPULAR CULTURE

Prior to the mid-1960s, African Americans appeared in popular culture as entertainers and athletes but were often portrayed in stereotypical roles on the stage, screen, and in popular media. Empowered by the Black cultural movement, African Americans increasingly demanded more substantial roles and genuine images of their lives, both in mainstream and Black media.

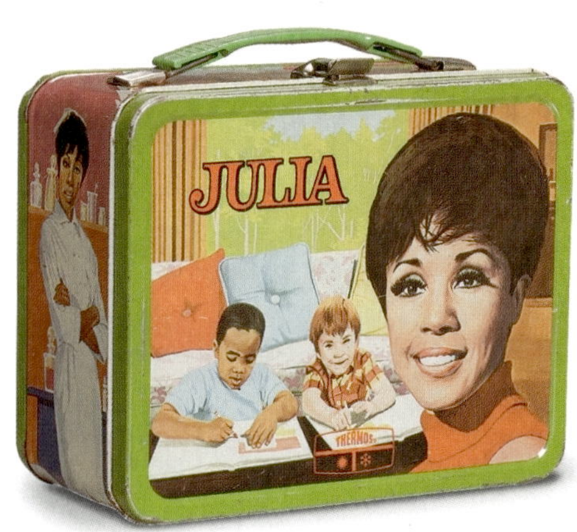

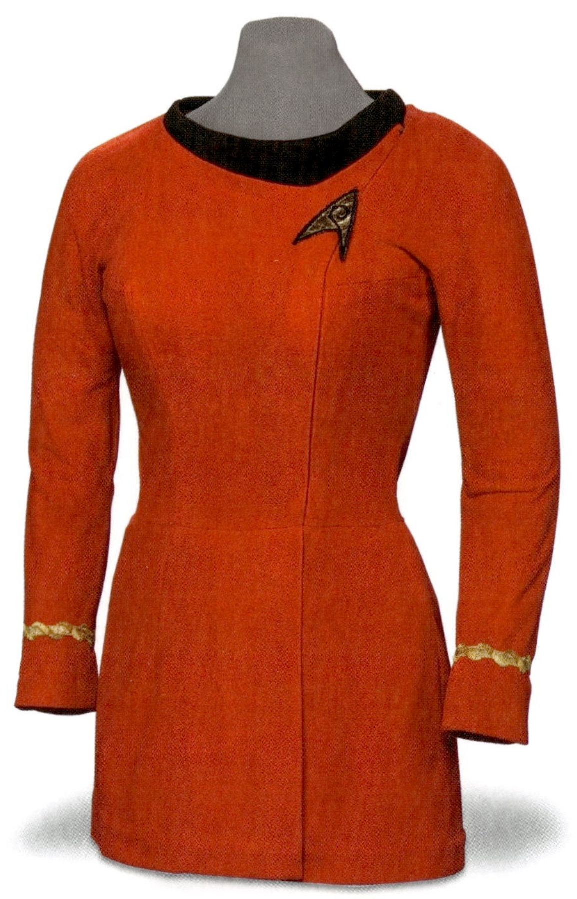

(*above*) This 1968 metal lunchbox is based on the television show *Julia*, starring Diahann Carroll in the titular role.

(*right*) Wearing this sleek red uniform, Nichelle Nichols starred as Lt. Nyota Uhura, chief communications officer of the USS *Enterprise* in *Star Trek*.

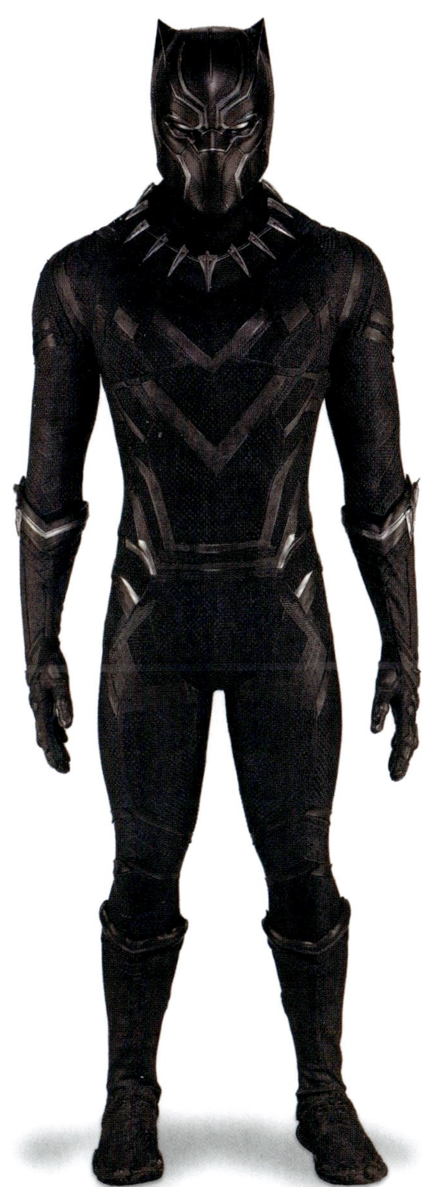

The Black Panther costume worn by actor Chadwick Boseman during the filming of the movie *Captain America: Civil War* (2016).

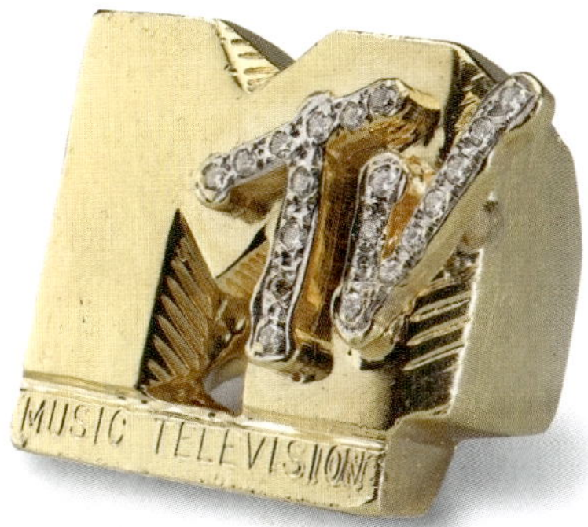

A gold and diamond MTV ring designed by Tito the Jeweler, aka "Manny," and owned by the hip-hop artist and pioneer Fab 5 Freddy.

THE PERFORMING ARTS

African American artists and performers developed various strategies to overcome the limitations society often placed on their creative freedom, opportunities, and identities. In 1959, Lorraine Hansberry's *A Raisin in the Sun* became the first all-Black Broadway play to win a New York Drama Critics Award.

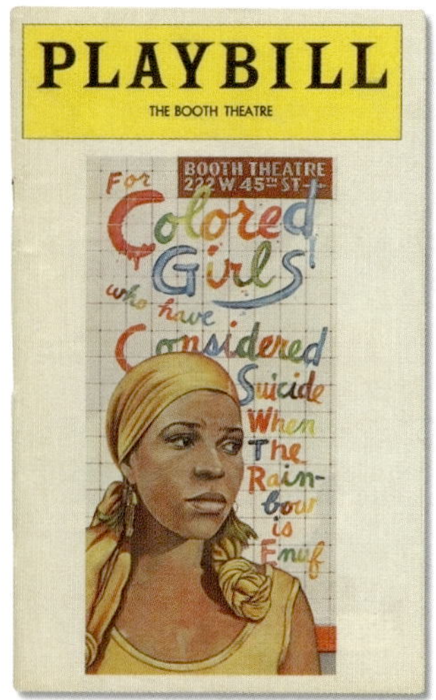

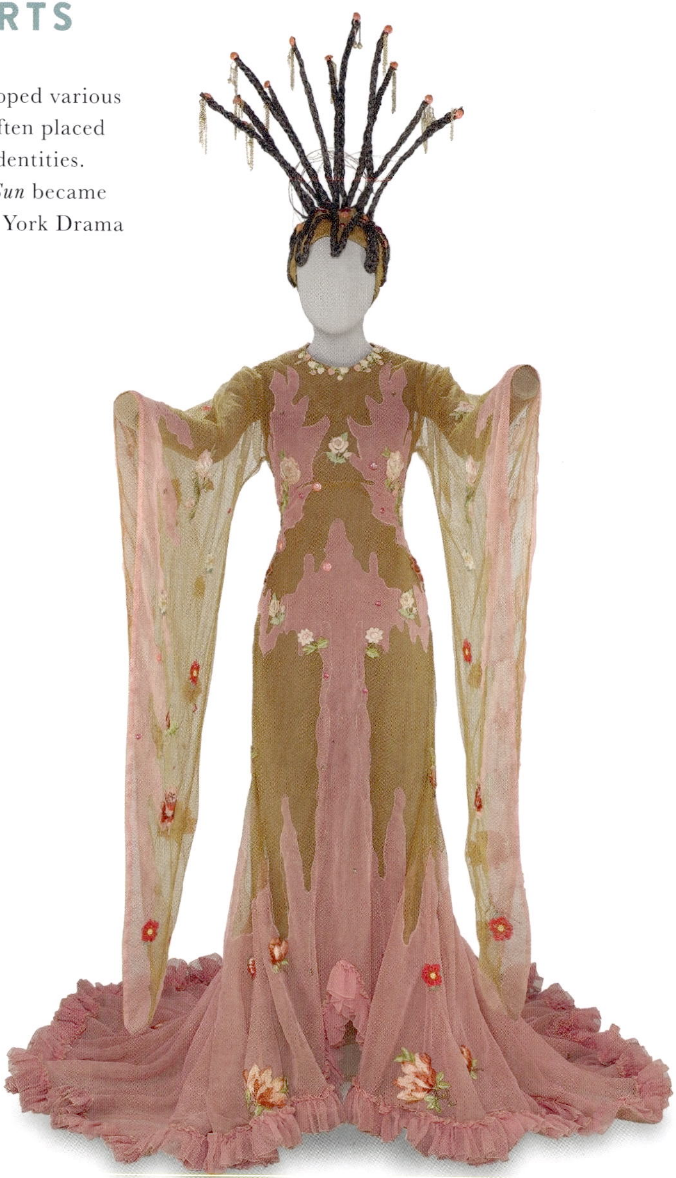

(*above*) A playbill from a November 1977 Broadway performance of *for colored girls who have considered suicide/when the rainbow is enuf* by Ntozake Shange at the Booth Theater.

(*right*) The costume designed by Geoffrey Holder and worn by Dee Dee Bridgewater in her Tony Award–winning performance as Glinda, the Good Witch, in the smash 1975 Broadway hit *The Wiz: The Super Soul Musical "Wonderful Wizard of Oz."*

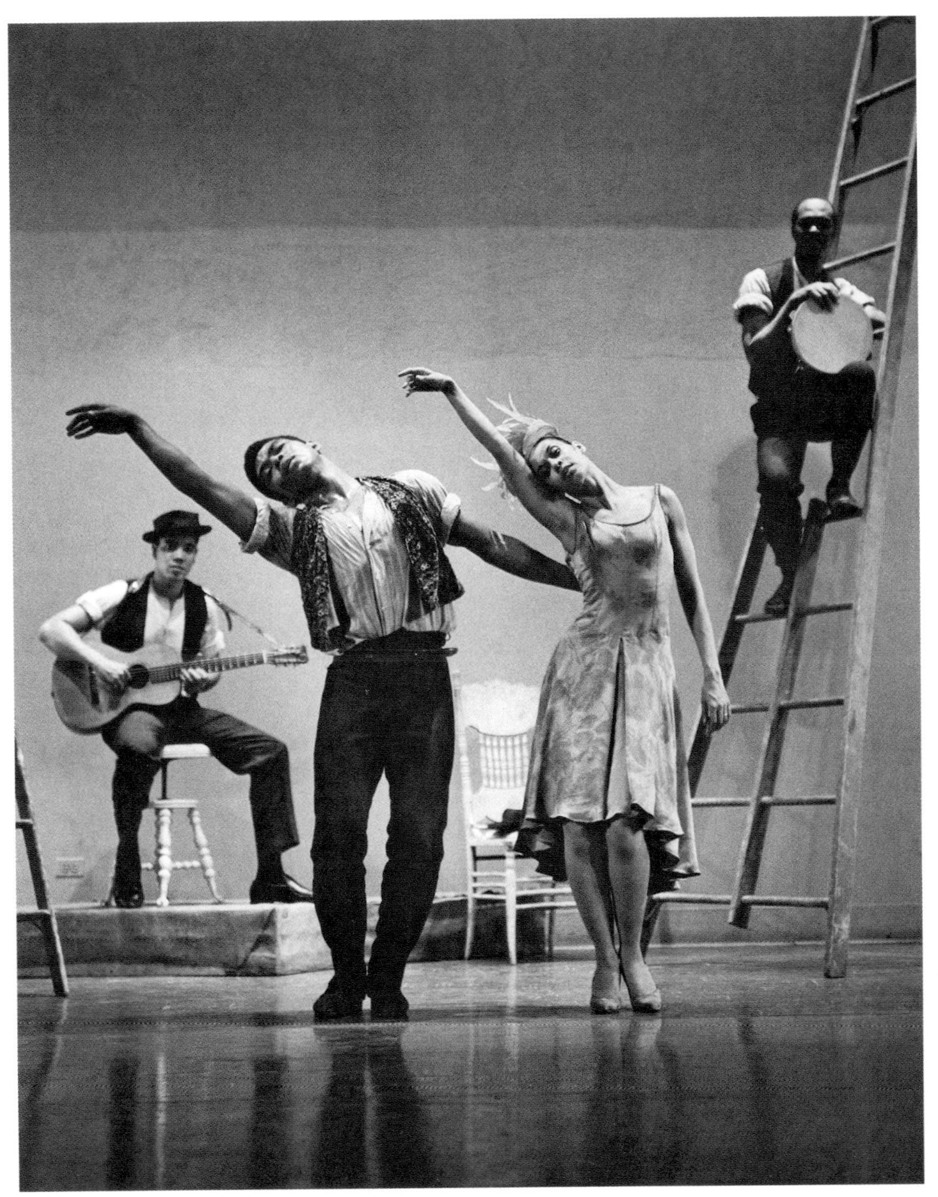

Alvin Ailey and Carmen De Lavallade are photographed by Jack Mitchell while performing *Roots of the Blues*, in Ailey's 1961 paean to African American musical traditions.

VISUAL ART

Like other American artists, Black artists in the nineteenth century worked in the European tradition. After World War I, however, some African American painters and sculptors explored their cultural roots and embraced more abstract forms and designs.

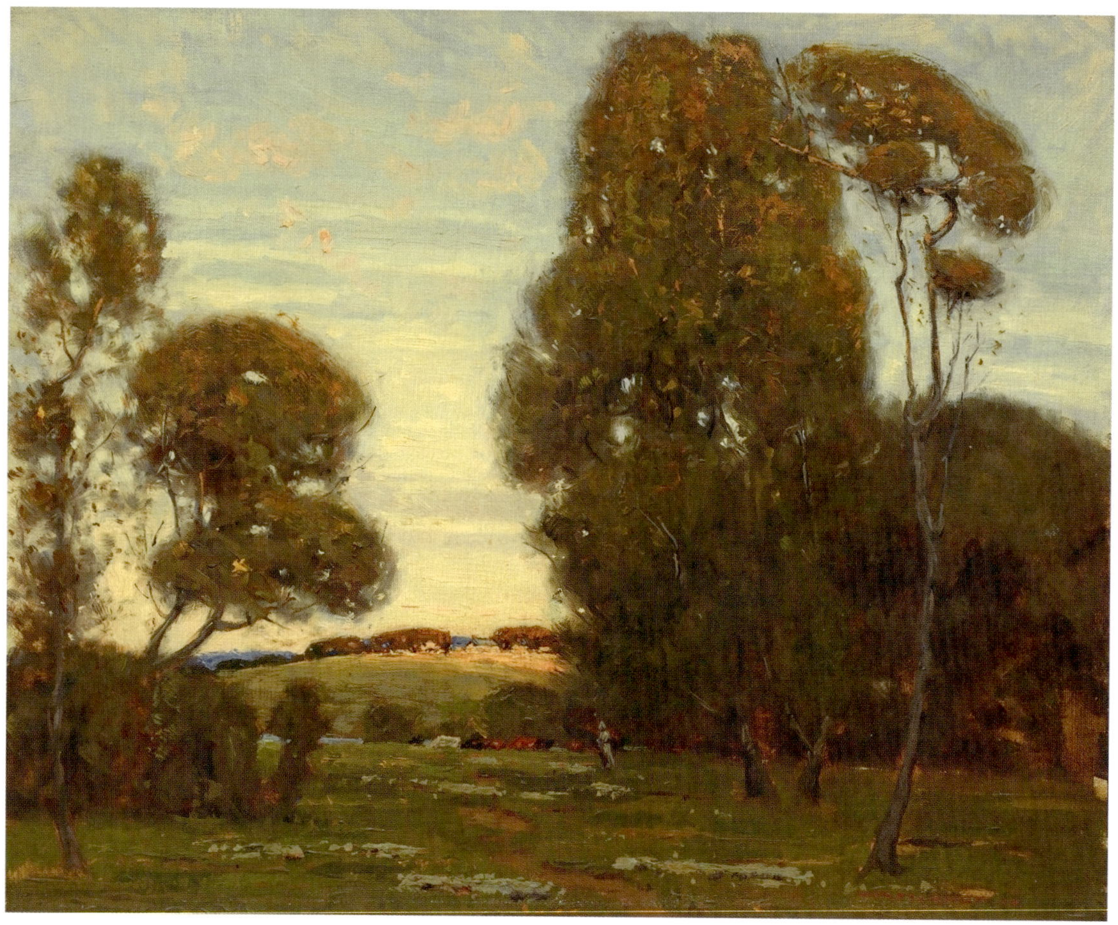

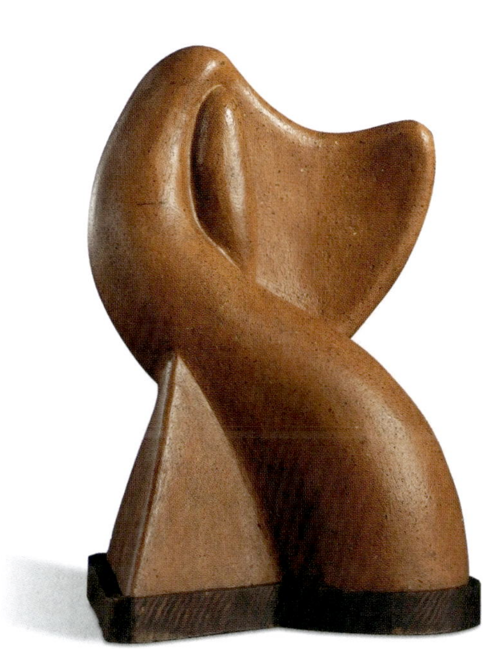

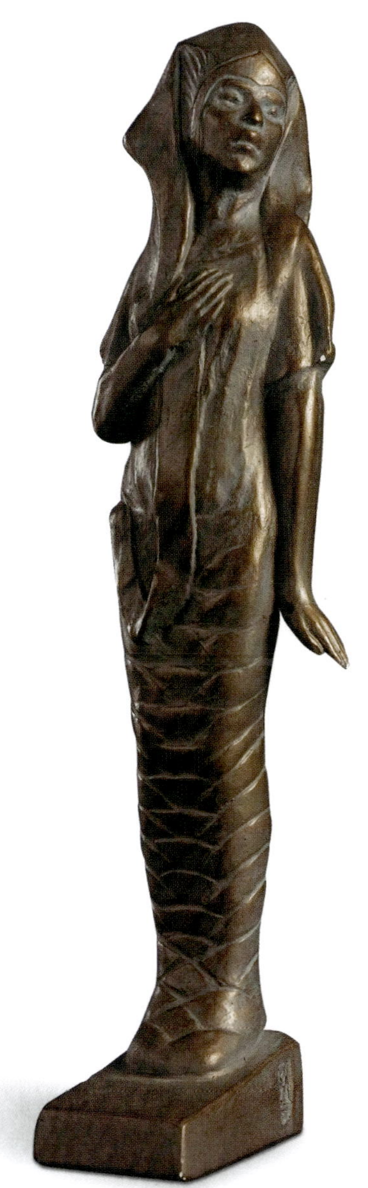

(*opposite*) William A. Harper, who studied in Paris as well as Chicago, painted this French rural scene in 1905.

(above) Dancer (1938–43) was sculpted by Sargent Claude Johnson, the first African American artist on the West Coast to achieve national recognition.

(*right*) Meta Vaux Warrick Fuller's *Ethiopia* (ca. 1921) symbolizes Africans shedding the bonds of enslavement and reawakening to their ancient heritage.

ART AND ACTIVISM

Protesting against social injustice can happen in the streets, but also in artists' studios. Artists have long used historical symbols and contemporary mediums to create images expressing outrage as well as hope, depicting resilience, and urging change.

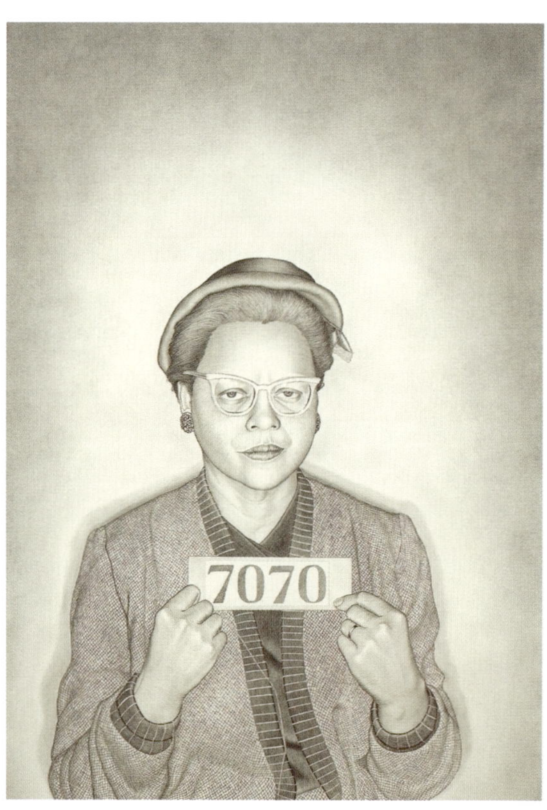

(*left*) Artist Lava Thomas created a series drawn from real mugshots of the brave women arrested during the Montgomery Bus Boycott in the 1950s, including this portrait of Euretta F. Adair (2018).

(*below*) In *Revolutionary* (1972), Wadsworth Jarrell portrays social and political activist Angela Davis using a complex and dynamic arrangement of color and her own words drawn from speeches and interviews.

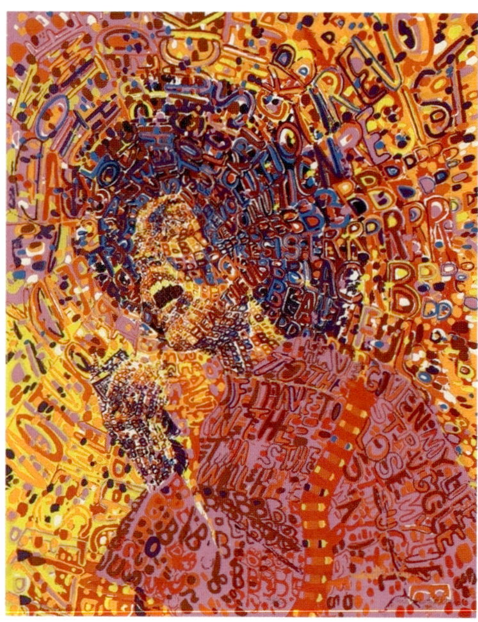

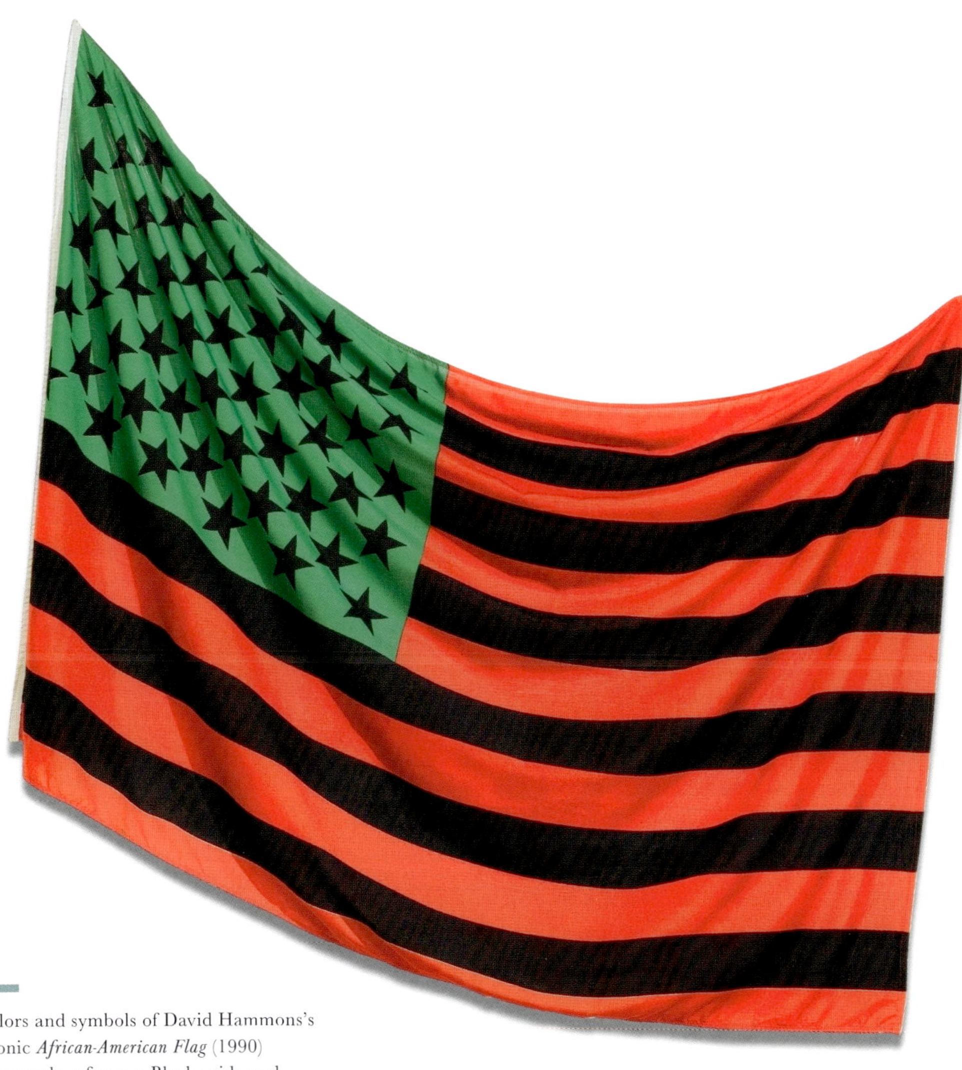

The colors and symbols of David Hammons's now-iconic *African-American Flag* (1990) simultaneously reference Black pride and heritage and the ways many African Americans celebrated freedom even as they endeavored to realize some of the nation's most profound, yet unfulfilled, promises.

This book may be purchased for educational, business, or sales promotional use. For information please write the Special Markets Department at the address or website below.

Published by Smithsonian Books
PO Box 37012, MRC 513
Washington, DC 20013
smithsonianbooks.com

Director: Carolyn Gleason
Senior Editor: Jaime Schwender
Production Editor: Julie Huggins
Digital Imaging Technician: Bill Whitcher

Edited by Robert A. Poarch
Designed by Leah Germann

National Museum of African American History and Culture
Deputy Director/Head of Publications: Michelle D. Commander
Senior Editor/Publications Manager: Douglas Remley
Writer/Editor: Julianna White
Publications Team: Emily Houf, Michèle Gates Moresi, Douglas Remley, and Kevin Strait

Library of Congress Control Number 2025033075

Paperback ISBN: 978-1-58834-813-5

Printed in China
Not at government expense

30 29 28 27 26 1 2 3 4 5

Picture Credits
Key: top (*t*), bottom (*b*), left (*l*), right (*r*), center (*c*)

Unless otherwise noted, all objects are from the collection of the Smithsonian National Museum of African American History and Culture.

Half title: Crowds reach back to the Washington Monument at the 1963 March on Washington for Jobs and Freedom.
Title: *Spring–Delightful Flower Bed* (1967), painting by Alma Thomas.

1: 2012.107.5, © Bruce Davidson/Magnum Photos
2: 2015.151, Gift of William J. and Brenda L. Galloway and Family, © Charles Thomas Lewis
5: Alan Karchmer/NMAAHC
7: (*tl*) 2015.190; (*r*) 2007.3.1ab, Gift of the Black Fashion Museum founded by Lois K. Alexander-Lane; (*cl*) 2023.106, Museum purchase generously supported by American Express, © Hank Willis Thomas. Courtesy of the artist and Jack Shainman Gallery, New York; (*b*) 2011.137.1, Donation of Charles E. Berry
8: 2013.57, Gift of The Edisto Island Historic Preservation Society, photograph by Eric Long/ Smithsonian Institution
9: (*t*) 2012.46.46; (*bl*) 2014.25, Gift of Elaine E. Thompson, in memory of Joseph Trammell, on behalf of his direct descendants; (*br*) 2010.27.1
10: 2010.14
11: 2011.69
12: (*l*) 2010.36.10ab; (*r*) 2014.151.3
13: (*tl*) 2014.115.9, Gift of the Garrison Family in memory of George Thompson Garrison; (*bl*) 2013.207.1; (*r*) 2007.6.1.17, © 2025 The Jacob and Gwendolyn Knight Lawrence Foundation, Seattle / Artists Rights Society (ARS), New York
14: (*l*) 2009.50.39, Gift of Charles L. Blockson; (*r*) 2017.30.47, Collection of the National Museum of African American History and Culture shared with the Library of Congress
15: 2009.50.25, Gift of Charles L. Blockson
16: (*l*) 2012.37ab, Gift of the Family of Irving and Estelle Liss; (*r*) 2012.133
17: (*t*) 2014.115.1.1ab, Gift of the Garrison Family in memory of George Thompson Garrison; (*bl*) 2010.24a-d; (*cr*) 2011.4.2ab
18: (*l*) 2010.77.7; (*tr*) 2012.40; (*br*) 2018.35.2.1ab
19: (*t*) 2013.168.1, Gift of the Family of William Beverly Nash; (*b*) 2020.10.9.2
20: (*cl*) 2011.35.2.50, Gift of Stephanie Capparell, author of *The Real Pepsi Challenge*; (*cr*) 2015.97.42; (*tr*) 2011.159.3.50, Gift from Dawn Simon Spears and Alvin Spears, Sr.; (*br*) 2012.46.31
21: (*l*) 2014.27.2, Gift of Ginette DePreist in memory of James DePreist; (*r*) 2013.208.2a-p, Gift of Dr. and Mrs. T.B. Boyd, III and R.H. Boyd Publishing Corporation
22: (*l*) 2010.2.2a-d; (*r*) TA2017.13.10.2, Gift of Ray and Jean Langston in memory of Mary Church and Robert Terrell
23: (*tl*) A2017.13.1.45, Gift of Ray and Jean Langston in memory of Mary Church and Robert Terrell; (*bl*) 2010.60.1.25, Frances Albrier Collection; (*cr*) 2022.21.22
24: (*l*) 2010.66.126, Gift of Jackie Bryant Smith; (*r*) 2014.63.63.1
25: (*tl*) 2014.63.63.33; (*bl*) 2014.63.63.31.1-.2; (*cl*) 2010.31.5, Gift of Kenneth Victor Young in memory of Thomas McCord, Louisville, Kentucky; (*tr towel*) 2012.46.75.3; (*tr hanger*) 2014.63.63.23.1; (*tr brush*) 2014.63.63.6; (*tr shoehorn*) 2012.75.2, Gift of Descendants of Robert and Georgia Thomas, Pulaski, Tenn.
26-27: SC.0031, Gift of Pete Claussen and Gulf and Ohio Railways
27: (*t*) James Di Loreto/Smithsonian Institution
28: (*l*) 2016.71ab, Gift of J. Wesley Huguley IV in memory of Dr. John W. Huguley III; (*tr*) 2017.111.9, Gift of Alan Laird; (*br*) 2022.42.1, Gift of Pia Marie Winters Jordan in memory of her mother, First Lieutenant Louise Virginia Lomax Winters, Army Nurse Corps; and her uncle, Sgt. Henry James Lomax, U.S. Army
29: (*t*) 2010.74.147, Gift of Joe Schwartz and Family, © Joe Schwartz; (*br*) 2015.97.24
30: 2011.82.1-.2, photograph by Michael R. Barnes/Smithsonian Institution
31: (*tl*) 2011.168; (*tr*) 2012.43.1, Gift of Lt. Col. Woodrow W. Crockett; (*br*) 2007.8
32: 2012.18.1, Gift of the Chicago Defender Publishing Company
33: (*tl*) 2012.84.11, Gift of Bobbie Ross in memory of Elizabeth Dillard; (*tr*) 2013.62.1, Gift of Mrs. Mary Churchwell and Dr. Kevin Churchwell and Mrs. Gloria Churchwell; (*br*) Johnson Publishing Company Archive. Courtesy J. Paul Getty Trust and Smithsonian National Museum of African American History and Culture. Made possible by the Ford Foundation, J. Paul Getty Trust, John D. and Catherine T. MacArthur Foundation, Andrew W. Mellon Foundation and Smithsonian Institution.
34: (*cl*) 2010.71.3, Gift from the Trumpauer-Mulholland Collection; (*tr*) 2013.201.1.23.3
34–35: 2009.16.9, © Ernest C. Withers Trust
35: (*tl*) 2013.138abc, Gift of the Family of Rev. Norman C. "Jim" Jimerson and Melva Brooks Jimerson; (*r*) 2012.117.1ab, Gift of Carlotta Walls LaNier
36: (*c*) 2017.6, Gift of Edith Lee-Payne and Family; (*b*) 2013.187.4, Gift of Samuel Y. Edgerton
37: 2021.67.6, Gift of Jim and Elise Blair, © Estate of James P. Blair
38: (*l*) 2012.28.2, Gift of Ellen Siegel; (*r*) 2011.58
39: (*l*) Johnson Publishing Company Archive. Courtesy J. Paul Getty Trust and Smithsonian National Museum of African American History and Culture. Made possible by the Ford Foundation, J. Paul Getty Trust, John D. and Catherine T. MacArthur Foundation, Andrew W. Mellon Foundation and Smithsonian Institution.; (*r*) 2014.167.3, Gifted with pride from Ellen Brooks
40: (*l*) 2015.254, © De Andrea Nichols, Marcis Curtis, Damon Davis, Sophie Lipman, Derek Laney, Mallory Nezam, Elizabeth Vega; (*br*) 2016.52.16, Gift of Zun Lee, © Zun Lee
41: (*t*) 2011.115.2, Gift of the Mid-Missouri Campaign Field Office, Columbia, MO; (*cl*) 2021.77.3, © Tony Mobley; (*br*) 2021.6.26, Courtesy of Stacey Y. Abrams, © Sowing Truth and Justice Collective
42: (*l*) 2014.30.3; (*r*) 2014.89.7.3
43: (*cl*) 2019.67.1, Gift of Neal Henderson, Founder and Coach of the Fort Dupont Hockey Program, © Fort Dupont Hockey Club; (*bl*) 2015.198ab, © Nike; (*tr*) 2016.38.1, Gift of Debra Janine Thomas
44: (*l*) 2012.154.32, Gift of Carl Lewis Estate; (*r*) 2019.28.39.3
45: (*cl*) 2023.96.4.1; (*c*) 2015.223.1ab, Gift of Rafer Johnson; (*cr*) 2015.58.5ab, Gift of Briana Scurry, © Nike; (*br*) 2016.35, Gift of the Rudolph Family in memory of Wilma Rudolph
46: (*cl*) 2019.22.9; (*bc*) 2014.218.1, Gift of Dooky Chase's Restaurant and Chef Leah Chase; (*tr*) 2017.82.3, Gift of Juliette Bethea in memory of Flora Wilson Bethea
47: (*l*) 2023.64.1, Design © Jomo Tariku; (*tr*) 2021.95.6, Gift of Peter Cook in honor of Julian Francis Abele and Julian Abele Cook, Sr.; (*br*) 2016.174.3, © Smithsonian National Museum of African American History and Culture
48: (*l*) 2021.38, purchased through the American Women's History Initiative Acquisitions Pool, administered by the Smithsonian American Women's History Initiative, © Bisa Butler; (*r*) 2014.276.1, Gift of Graham Holdings Company, © 2025 Mensie Lee Pettway/ Artists Rights Society (ARS), New York
49: (*tl*) 2012.155.10, Gift of the Lyles Station Historic Preservation Corporation; (*br*) 2013.162.7
50: (*tl*) 2013.213.9; (*br*) 2010.6.45, Gift from Mae Reeves and her children, Donna Limerick and William Mincey, Jr.; (*tr*) 2016.48.11ab, Gift of Donna Limerick; (*br*) 2013.213.6
51: (*bl*) Johnson Publishing Company Archive. Courtesy J. Paul Getty Trust and Smithsonian National Museum of African American History and Culture. Made possible by the Ford Foundation, J. Paul Getty Trust, John D. and Catherine T. MacArthur Foundation, Andrew W. Mellon Foundation and Smithsonian Institution. (*r*) 2007.3.19, Gift of the Black Fashion Museum founded by Lois K. Alexander-Lane
52: (*l*) 2019.10.1a-g; (*cr*) 2010.54.4; (*br*) 2014.98.7, Gift of Gayle Wald
53: (*tl*) 2022.21.17; (*c*) 2020.27.3.1-.2; (*r*) 2021.92.2a-f, Donated by Vernon Reid
54: (*l*) 2011.96; (*r*) 2014.37.46
55: (*l*) 2022.21.16; (*r*) 2020.26.36
56: (*l*) 2013.108.13ab, © 1969 Savannah Productions. Inc.; (*r*) 2016.126
57: (*l*) 2018.39.1.1abc-.5ab, Gift of Marvel Studios and The Walt Disney Company, © Marvel; (*r*) 2020.38.6
58: (*l*) 2012.152.1213, Gift of Dow B. Ellis, Playbill used by permission. All rights reserved, © Playbill Inc.; (*r*) 2007.3.11, Gift of the Black Fashion Museum founded by Lois K. Alexander-Lane
59: A2013.245.1.2.3.21, Photography by Jack Mitchell, © Alvin Ailey Dance Foundation, Inc. and Smithsonian Institution, All rights reserved.
60: 2010.51.1ab
61: (*l*) 2013.164; (*r*) 2013.242.1, Gift of the Fuller Family, © Meta Vaux Warrick Fuller
62: (*l*) 2021.55, Gift of Cheryl and Charles Ward, © Lava Thomas; (*r*) 2010.3.1, © Wadsworth Jarrell
63: 2022.7, Partial gift of Jan Christiaan Braun, who curated the ground-breaking exhibition *Black USA* in Amsterdam in 1990, for which the *African-American Flag* was created. Museum purchase supported by The Ford Foundation and the Andrew W. Mellon Foundation. © 2025 David Hammons / Artists Rights Society (ARS), New York